**Dear Reader,**

The book you are holding is one of the books of IIMA Business Books series published in collaboration with Random House to disseminate knowledge to executives in a manner that brings them up to date in different fields of management. The first set of books in the series published in 2010 and 2011 were liked immensely by the readers. Several of the books went on to become best-sellers. The set was expanded further in 2012 with publication of books on new topics. The idea is to publish books on a comprehensive list of topics in management over time for practising managers. These books are written by authors who have rich experience of teaching executives from a diverse set of organizations. Written in a conversational style with numerous illustrations from the world of practice, you would find the books useful in your work life. The references cited in the books provide you with ready information on where to look for more detailed knowledge on specific topics and concepts.

The financial market crisis of 2007–08 and the resulting economic downturn since then are still impacting economies all over the world. The common man has been left puzzled by the events as he is unable to comprehend the *Ashani Sanket* that destroyed his orderly world. The book *Day to Day Economics* explains the factors that impact the economic well-being of individuals due to what institutions and governments do and do not do. Written in a lucid style, with glossary of words and phrases at the end of each chapter, the book demystifies arcane concepts in economics for the reader. The author engages the reader's attention with illustrations and stories from other fields, including the duel between Adi Shankaracharya and Bharati. The crossword puzzle on economics at the end of the book is an added unexpected attraction for the readers to unobtrusively test their understanding of principles of economics. I am certain that you will enjoy reading the book while unravelling the distant economic thunders that impact your day-to-day life.

Write to us suggesting topics that you would like covered in the books that are to be published under the series in the future.

**Samir K. Barua**
Director
IIM Ahmedabad

INDIA'S BESTSELLING BUSINESS BOOKS SERIES

# DAY TO DAY
# ECONOMICS

**INDIA'S BESTSELLING BUSINESS BOOKS SERIES**

# IIM
AHMEDABAD
BUSINESS BOOKS

# DAY TO DAY
# ECONOMICS

## SATISH Y. DEODHAR

RANDOM BUSINESS

RANDOM BUSINESS

USA | Canada | UK | Ireland | Australia
New Zealand | India | South Africa | China

Random Business is part of the Penguin Random House group of companies
whose addresses can be found at global.penguinrandomhouse.com

Published by Penguin Random House India Pvt. Ltd
7th Floor, Infinity Tower C, DLF Cyber City,
Gurgaon 122 002, Haryana, India

Penguin
Random House
India

First published by Random House India 2012

26  25  24

ISBN  9788184001631

Typeset in Sabon by Eleven Arts
Printed at Replika Press Pvt. Ltd, India

www.penguin.co.in

*To my mother,*
*the Gangotri of what I am today,*

*and*

*to my late father,*
*the most 'civil' engineer I have ever met!*

# CONTENTS

# CONTENTS

# PREFACE

Quite a few reasons prompted me to write this book. On various occasions, when friends, family folk, and acquaintances come to know that I teach economics, invariably their immediate reaction is a sense of spatial and mental estrangement! Perhaps this happens with most economists, for economics has got a reputation of being an esoteric social science which doesn't have much in common with real life. Nothing can be further from the truth and it has been my dream to prove it. Hence, the character of this book has been shaped by a missionary zeal to convert. At the Indian Institute of Management, Ahmedabad (IIMA), economics is taught in the short-duration executive programmes in management and in the post-graduate programmes in management. However, we often find that conveying and understanding theoretical concepts and relating them to the Indian economy in a short period of time is a very challenging task, both for the faculty and the participants in the programmes. Therefore, the subject needs to be tackled with a different approach, and the interrelationships between the economic institutions and the economic phenomena that pervade our lives need to be taught by using lots of everyday examples. This book addresses that need.

There have been quite a few teachers and colleagues who have had an influence in shaping the direction of my academic career. They include high-school teachers like Bhalerao Sir, who aroused my curiosity in economics by teaching *Ghatatya Upabhogyatecha Siddhanta* or the law of diminishing marginal utility; and Datar Sir, who used to bring models to the classroom to show celestial phenomena, such as, eclipses and the phases of the moon. At the Gokhale Institute of Politics and Economics, Pune, Mrs Sulabha Sidhaye took the fear of English out of my psyche, and Professor Nilakantha Rath gave a solid grounding in economics. At The Ohio State University, my PhD guide, Professor Ian Sheldon, brought discipline into my academic writing. Later, when I entered IIMA as a complete stranger, colleagues, such as, Professors Sasi Mishra, Gopal Naik, Devanath Tirupati, Ravindra Dholakia, and Samar Datta, influenced my academic progress. Finally, IIMA Directors gave me the opportunities to serve as Warden, PGP Admissions Chairperson, first Convener of the computerized Common Admission Test (CAT), and Chairperson of PGPX programme. This book is a tribute to all of them.

# ACKNOWLEDGEMENTS

In the course of writing this book, I have received warm support from ten people. It is my pleasure to thank them on this page. The process of writing a book needs a catalyst to initiate the process. Professor Samir Barua, in his capacity as Director of IIMA, played that role when he introduced me to Chiki Sarkar of Random House. Subsequently, Chiki and I sat down to chalk out the plan of the book. Her suggestions on the chapter scheme and writing style which would appeal to a reader with no economics background were very helpful. When about a third of the book was completed, she left Random House and I too got quite involved in teaching, Equis accreditation work, and the administrative chores of a PGPX chairperson. The spirit of writing almost flagged and that is when Milee Ashwarya brought in encouragement at a critical moment of despondency. In the concluding stages, Radhika Marwah helped me to complete the book, Meena Bhende refined the writing with her copy-editing, and Avinash Jai Singh designed a wonderful cover. My sincere thanks to all six of them.

Amey Sapre, my good-natured research associate, did everything that was foisted on him, which included collection of data, vital statistics, and referencing. Special thanks to him for his support. And how can I forget my immediate family? As if being an immaculate homemaker and simultaneously pursuing a master's degree in Indian classical music were not difficult enough, my wife, Deepali, willingly took over many of my household responsibilities as I began sprinting towards the completion of this book. Sylee, my 10th-grader daughter would be fully justified in complaining of my unavailability for clarifying her doubts during her crucial board exam year. However, she showed a heightened sense of maturity and patience by waiting for mutually opportune spare time. My son Yash, too, missed out on a few cricket duels in our backyard and on listening to a story or two at bedtime. But he never grumbled. Deepali, Sylee, and Yash—thanks for accommodating me.

# INTRODUCTION

'If there's a book you really want to read but it hasn't been written yet, then you must write it.'

—TONI MORRISON

Have you been wondering why food prices have skyrocketed in the past few years? When you were planning to secure a loan to buy a car, a home, or a piece of machinery for your business, didn't your friends or business colleagues tell you to wait, for interest rates on loans were expected to fall? And, till only a few years ago, industries were laying off workers the world over. India was no exception. Did you wonder why some of your acquaintances who had just graduated then were finding it difficult to get a job with a decent remuneration? And, later, even when things began to look much better for you and your acquaintances, you may still have occasionally asked yourself while waiting at a traffic light: Why does a kid in ragged clothes still have to knock on your car window and beg you to buy balloons for a pittance?

In one's role as a homemaker or a breadwinner, a student or a professional, a businessperson or an employee, one seeks answers to these and many other economic questions. If you are one such person with an inquiring mind, this book is for you. You will find it interesting because it discusses the economic environment that is so intricately linked with the managing of everyday business decisions, both of households and firms.

The term 'economics' comes from the Ancient Greek word *oikonomia* (*oikos*, house + *nomos*, custom or law), meaning 'rules or management of a household'. One finds reference to these words in the Socratic dialogue on household management and agriculture. Another reference is attributed to Aristotle's work titled *Oikonomikos*. About the same time, that is, circa 327 BCE, the Indian statesman Kautilya also wrote a treatise, *Arthashastra*, in which he describes economics as the basis for attaining material goods and spiritual good. However, economics, in its modern form, attained visibility when Adam Smith wrote his famous treatise, *An Inquiry into the Nature and Causes of the Wealth of Nations* in 1776. Since then, economics has evolved into an analytical modern social science with applications in practically all spheres of life. One of the branches of economics that focuses on individual economic decisions of households and firms is called microeconomics. Another—which focuses on understanding the changes in the aggregate business environment—is called macroeconomics. The development and importance of this social science was firmly recognized when the Nobel Memorial Prize in Economic Sciences was instituted in 1968.

Despite the progress made in economics, a few people still perceive it as a dismal science. To paraphrase Paul Krugman, the winner of the Nobel Memorial Prize in Economic Sciences in 2008, those who plan to go into business often major in economics but only a few believe that what they learn in economics will help them run a business. One of the reasons for this bleak impression is the expectation and the misconception that economics equips one with immediate, direct, hands-on tools to run a business. The reality is that the principles of microeconomics form the basis for developing concepts in consumer- and business-related subjects such as finance, marketing, banking, governance, and others. The second reason is that students of economics often ignore the fact that macroeconomics equips one with a sound understanding of the economic environment in which a consumer or a business operates. Perhaps, the importance of knowing the business environment is understood years after leaving college, for only then does one begin to make serious economic decisions—personal or professional. Finally, of course, it also matters whether or not economics is made interesting in the classroom by relating it to market institutions and the environment in which a consumer or a business operates. Though there are exceptions, more often than not, the application part tends to get ignored.

'If there's a book you really want to read but it hasn't been written yet, then you must write it,' said Toni Morrison, a Nobel laureate who worked with Random House. This book is designed precisely to overcome the perceived inaccessibility of economics to consumers and businesses alike. Hence, the reader is not presented with yet another typical, stylized textbook in economics. Rather, it is hoped that the reader— whether an entrepreneur, a homemaker, or a student—will gain a contextual understanding of the application of economic principles through exposure to the various institutions and phenomena that pervade our economic life. By no means is this exposure to institutions, economic phenomena, and economic principles complete, but an attempt has been made to offer a platter of select important topics that concern us as an economic man (*homo economicus*).

This book begins with introducing us to key economic institutions within which we operate. We know that the government does intervene in the market and, many times, engages in certain activities which you may have wondered why private firms do not—or are not allowed to—undertake. For example, you will get clues as to why only the government offers defence services, or why it should not engage itself in producing watches! This issue is addressed in Chapter 1. If the government intervenes in the market or undertakes some economic activities, it needs to manage finances for such activities. Are the government's budget deficits bad for us? Is lowering income tax a good thing for us? Chapter 2 takes up these issues and describes the nature of the government's budget, taxes, and financial deficits. Two other important institutions with which we are closely associated are banks and stock markets. How are the fluctuations in stock prices related to the health of industry? Why would banks not have, at any point in time, sufficient cash to pay all its deposit-holders? These are questions we address in Chapter 3. Suppose you are a very good computer programmer and an excellent entrepreneur as well. Would you not then start your own firm? You may hire someone who is a good programmer but not so good an entrepreneur. What is true between individuals is also true between countries. It is this principle of comparative advantage that forms the basis of the formation of the World Trade Organization (WTO). We will address the economic rationale and the status of WTO negotiations in Chapter 4.

Then, we will cover a few economic phenomena that affect all of us directly. In the recent past, prices of all goods in general and food in particular have been rising rapidly in India. For example, why is it that the pulses, the staple source of protein for Indians, have become so expensive? Such concerns are addressed in Chapter 5, where we try to understand the causes, consequences, and remedies for general price rise—commonly known as inflation. Economies go through the cycle of boom and bust. If inflation is worrisome sometimes then some other times are characterized by a general difficulty to find jobs and lower profits for the firms. Why is it that bombing of the World Trade Centre can cause such a situation? And why is it that applications to post-graduate programmes may rise during such periods? We will be able to answer such questions when we discuss the phenomenon of recession in Chapter 6. We will also discuss the two major policies that are used to cure recessions—fiscal policy and monetary policy. It is true that despite the severe recession the world over, India fared better compared to most during the recent past. The Indian economy has been growing at about an average growth rate of more than 7 percent for a decade now. However, despite this fact, one does see substantive deprivation and poverty among the masses in India. Is the economic growth inclusive in nature or does it show unaimed opulence? We look at this issue in Chapter 7. Finally concluding observations are made in Chapter 8. Key economic terms are defined in the Ready Reckoner at the end of each chapter.

## REFERENCES:

Eatwell, J., Milgate, M. and Newman, P., (1987), 'The New Palgrave: A Dictionary of Economics,' London: Macmillan

Kangle, R.P., (1986), *Kautiliya Arthashastra*, Vols. 1–3, Delhi: Motilal Banarasidas

Krugman, P., (1996), 'A Country is Not a Company,' Harvard Business Review, Jan-Feb

Smith, A., (1776), *An Inquiry into the Nature and Causes of the Wealth of Nations*, Oxford World's Classics, New York: Oxford University Press, Reissued in 2008

# CHAPTER 1

# MEDLEY OF GOVERNMENT AND PRIVATE SECTOR

*'We do not defend the perversions of the natural economic system; but because they are perversions merely, we shall remove them and keep the system.'*

—JOHN BATES CLARK

## THE ROLE OF THE GOVERNMENT

The institution known as government that is chosen by a people varies in its manifestations in different countries, and can vary from democracy to autocracy. Its basic function, whatever its form, remains the same—to define the rights as well as the obligations of citizens and to secure them by enacting and enforcing laws. The government enacts laws; its judiciary metes out judgments if those laws are violated; its police force maintains law and order; and its defence services offer protection from external aggression. Once this congenial framework is provided by the government to its people, market forces ensure the production and exchange of goods and services, leading to an efficient allocation and usage of resources.

One is aware that the private sector offers zillions of goods and services in the market. Interestingly, however, one finds that many economic activities, such as, power generation, water supply, roads, and postal services, are offered by the government. In fact, the government, going beyond the free market forces, is also involved in formulating policies to try and curtail unemployment and to control inflation. One would expect the economic activities which the government undertakes to be distinct from those undertaken by the private sector. However, the experience of the last several decades shows that the government has undertaken diverse activities such as manufacturing watches, bread, and offering air transport services—the same services which the private sector also provides. Thus, there is a medley of goods and services that are offered by the government and the private sector. Which principles, then, decide the distribution of economic activities between the government and the private sector? Is the overlap justified? The following discussion should shed light on the matter.

Some of you may have personally watched the spectacle at the Wagah border that separates India and Pakistan in the state of Punjab. The macho, competitive 'Beating Retreat' ceremony, enacted daily by soldiers on either side of the border is orchestrated by the armies of the two governments.

Why are defence services provided only by governments? Is it that soldiers demonstrate patriotism and bravery only when they work for the government? Or are the reasons more fundamental? When we see a postage stamp, we wonder what the picture and the wording represent. There is a tremendous diversity in stamps in terms of images, colours, language, currency, denominations, and the countries that issue them. But there is one thing common to all postage stamps—they are issued by governments. Stamps represent the price paid by a customer for a postal service that is rendered by the government. While private courier services are gaining ground, the service of delivering ordinary postcards, inland letters, aerograms, and money orders, to and from every nook and corner of India, is still provided by the government. Why has the private sector not entered this market? Or, does the government not permit it to enter?

We will try to find answers to such and similar questions by drawing attention to market failures that arise due to various factors such as non-rivalry in consumption, non-excludability, natural monopoly, and externalities. Once you understand these concepts, you will have a touchstone: a touchstone to help you judge whether or not certain economic activities undertaken by the government are justifiable or not.

## PURE PUBLIC GOODS

For a moment, travel back in time to your high-school days. On a lazy Saturday afternoon, to refresh yourself from the boring homework, you stand in the balcony of your apartment seeking inspiration. Suddenly, you hear the beating of drums on the street below: a street performer and his wife are inviting you to watch their acrobatic show. You, along with neighbours in other balconies, and a few others on the street—passive spectators, one and all—stand watching the performance. Once the show is over, the spectators disperse. The husband-and-wife team now looks up at each balcony, silently pleading for a few rupees. At that instant, you get a reality check. You run inside and sheepishly ask your parents whether or not you should give something to the couple. It is safe to assume that the performing couple barely makes two ends meet. No wonder, then, that street-performing is vanishing as a profession!

The performing couple is working hard to operate a private enterprise but, somehow, market forces fail to deliver even a bare minimum profit to the couple. Why do you think this happens? If you closely study this incident, you may identify the two factors that lead to market failure. One is the non-rivalry in consumption—you watched the street performance, but you did not prevent others from viewing it, too. Thus, there was no rivalry in the consumption of the service among different consumers. That is not so with other goods, say, a car or a toothpaste. If you buy a car, that same car is not available to anyone else. In other words, there is rivalry and competition among consumers which forces them to pay a price to secure possession of a car. The second factor is this: at a given market price, the relative buying power of different consumers might exclude some of them from buying the car or the toothpaste. In the case of the street-performing couple, this 'excludability' feature is missing, because they cannot prevent individuals—either physically or by charging an appropriate price—from viewing the performance. Thus, due to the non-rivalry and the non-excludability of the service which they provide, the problem of free riding occurs, and the market fails to deliver—ergo, the street performers cannot run a profitable business.

There are several instances of services that are non-rival in consumption and non-excludable. Such services are termed 'pure public goods'. The above examples will, perhaps, make clear to you why national defence is a pure public good. A private firm just cannot provide national defence profitably, for the consumption of this service is non-rival and non-excludable. On the individual level, why would anyone express how much they value their security, and why would anyone pay for it, when they can have a free ride at the expense of other consumers? It follows, then, that the market will fail to deliver, making it necessary for the central government of the country to provide national defence. The same idea can be extended to various activities, such as, the police force, low-traffic rural roads, lighthouses, street lights, among others. Private firms will not offer these services, because the free market cannot provide the required environment for making a profit. In this sense, the market fails to deliver these services, and the institution of government has to undertake these economic activities. Even in hard-core capitalist economies, these services are provided by the

## Of Lighthouses, Club Goods, and Prospects for Street Performers

Lighthouses warn ships at sea. They are typically characterized as public goods, for the service they provide is non-rival and non-excludable. Therefore, most lighthouses are owned by governments. One economist, Ronald Coase, has pointed out that some lighthouses in England used to be privately owned. These privately-owned lighthouses would charge the ships at nearby ports a fee for providing them with docking facilities at the port. It was possible for lighthouses situated near the ports to create excludability, that is, refrain from providing a service if a consumer refused to pay. Having obviously used the lighthouse for navigation, a ship would risk denial of docking facility if it declined to pay for lighthouse service. Thus, we see that, when excludability is brought in, it is possible for a private enterprise to provide a public good profitably. Such goods are called 'club goods'. As the name suggests, many social clubs which cater to high society restrict membership and charge high fees. This creates excludability and retains non-rivalry in the use of facilities such as swimming pools and gymnasiums. Is it possible for the street-performing couple discussed earlier take a cue from club goods? Yes. An enterprising trapeze artist who starts his own circus does exactly that—creates excludability. Now, can you think of other possibilities—an economic activity that involves non-excludability as well as rivalry in consumption?

government. Can you think of other such services? The next time you are waiting at a traffic signal, take a moment to look around you—have you ever seen a private operator deliver traffic signal service to commuters? But, of course, now you are in the driver's seat—you know that traffic signals are a pure public good!

## NATURAL MONOPOLIES

The marketplace is a medley of public sector and private sector operations. While the private sector produces most goods and services efficiently, economic activities which are in the nature of pure public good are delivered by the government. But governments also deliver other goods and services even if they are not pure public goods. For more than a decade now, private firms have been selling bottled potable water. Consumers have quickly accepted this offering from the private sector. Perhaps, this reflects the failure of local governments to supply safe, potable water through the network of municipal pipes and taps that runs through all households. But then, why don't private entities undertake the supply of potable water to the cities by setting up their own extensive network of pipes, taps, and water purification plants? Imagine several private firms establishing huge water purification plants and an extensive network of water pipes and taps all over the city! Not only would the capital cost of such networks be too high, there would also be a duplication of such networks with different private firms competing to offer this service. This duplication of networks is impractical.

Even if some firms were willing to undertake it, they would incur high costs and the customer base would get divided among the competing firms. As a result, the per-unit cost of delivering water would be extremely high.

The per-unit cost of delivering potable tap water would come down only if a single firm were to offer this service. That way, there would be no duplication of capital costs, and the capital cost for a single operator would get distributed over the large volume of water delivered. This implies that there is room only for a single firm—that is, a monopoly. However, if only a single private firm were allowed to offer this service, it would turn into a monopolist! In the absence of competition from other players, a profit-maximizing monopolist would charge a high price for water delivery, and the quantity supplied would also be quite low compared to what it would have been under competitive conditions. Goods and services that fall into this category are called 'natural monopolies'. Governments avoid the dilemma of such natural monopolies by undertaking these activities themselves and charging a low average price which would be close to the competitive price. The same logic can be extended to the nationwide governmental postal service. Establishing an extensive network of post offices throughout the length and breadth of a country of continental proportions is an apt example of a natural monopoly. As in the case of potable bottled water, taking advantage of improvements in communications technology, courier services are now competing with the government postal service. However, the delivery of ordinary

## Something to Ponder

In its effort to correct market failures, the Indian government created many public sector undertakings (PSUs) and nationalized quite a few privately owned firms. It has had a foothold in diverse sectors, such as, bakery, watches, machine tools, civil aviation, and hotels, to name a few. Many of these PSUs, if not all, are making heavy losses. Based on the arguments made earlier regarding market failures, do you think the government of India made the right decisions in establishing or nationalizing firms in the sectors mentioned above?

The proof of the pudding is in the eating. The government of India began the process of disinvestment of PSUs from 1991. In fact, disinvestment, through strategic sale, commenced in 1999–2000, when twelve PSUs and several hotel properties were disinvested. This included Modern Food Industries Ltd, a PSU that used to manufacture bread. This disinvestment process is expected to continue. As of now, among others, two of the most visible names—Air India and Hindustan Machines Tools (HMT)—continue to operate as PSUs and to make losses. The cumulative losses of Air India, as of the financial year 2010–11, were more than Rs 20,320 crore and government has decided to help Air India with an additional equity of Rs. 30,0000 crore over a nine year period. As a consumer, would you prefer HMT watches and Air India flights to other watches and other airlines simply because they are government-owned? Do they address the market failure concerns at all?

postcards, inland letters, and money orders to-and-from every nook and corner of the country still remains a natural monopoly. Government post offices and private couriers can exist simultaneously, at least until further improvements in communication technology reach the masses.

It is this same feature of natural monopoly that enables governments to own and run other activities, such as, the generation and supply of electricity, and the provision of landline telephone services. These natural monopolies are referred to in common parlance as 'public utilities' or, simply, utilities. Unfortunately, the track record of state electricity boards, state-owned telephone companies, and other state-owned natural monopolies is very poor. This condition emanates from the lack of incentives to the employees to offer better services, and the absence of a profit motive to judge the performance of the enterprise. It is for this reason that Lee Iacocca, former head of the Chrysler Corporation, once said, 'One of the things the government can't do is run anything. The only things our government runs are the post office and the railroads, and both of them are bankrupt.' While this statement may be too uncharitable, governments are not blind to such concerns. Therefore, governments often allow private monopolies to run utilities as long as their pricing and output levels are regulated by the government. Some firms, such as, Tata Power (Mumbai) and Torrent Power (Ahmedabad), are examples of private firms running electric utilities very efficiently, but their pricing and output decisions are regulated by the state electricity regulatory commissions.

# EXTERNALITIES

So far, we have looked at two features—public goods and natural monopolies—as the raison d'être for the government to undertake economic activities in the marketplace. However, there is one more reason why the government may interfere in the free market, if not undertake the economic activity itself. This happens when economic activities are characterized by what is known in economics as 'externality'. Externality occurs when a specific economic activity—production, consumption, or trade—affects a bystander who is not party to the specific economic activity. For example, late-night playing of loud music at festival pandals disturbs the peace in the neighbourhood. This form of celebration creates a negative externality on bystanders, namely, the residents of the neighbourhood. In the presence of a negative externality, the social cost of playing music is much higher than the private cost of playing music and renting equipment. Therefore, a city commissioner may intervene and put a limit on the decibel levels of the music, and ban music in public places after a certain time in the late evening.

Recently, the central government announced a subsidy of 20 percent on the production of the latest version of the electric car Reva. Why would a government give a subsidy to the manufacturing of electric cars? When consumers buy Reva, some private benefit accrues to them through its usage. Moreover, since this car is electric, it does not pollute the atmosphere—as do other cars. Besides, it avoids the use of petroleum—one of the earth's non-renewable resources.

Therefore, the social benefit of manufacturing Reva includes the benefit to the consumer, along with the value attached to lower pollution and to resource conservation. The social benefit of the electric car far exceeds the private benefit to the consumer. This means that there is a positive externality enjoyed by society when an individual buys a Reva. The government would certainly want to encourage more production of Reva and, hence, it offers a subsidy so that more such cars (and fewer petrol-driven cars) are manufactured and bought. If the government does not help, the market will fail to increase the number of environment-friendly cars, the pollution will be high, and a non-renewable resource will get depleted.

For a similar reason, the government has engaged itself in subsidizing primary education. The benefits of education go far beyond the private benefit accruing to a child. Education creates mature and responsible individuals who can effectively participate in the socio-economic development of society. Hence, by subsidizing education, citizens are incentivized to send their children to school, and educational trusts are encouraged to establish such schools. This, too, is an example of market failure, for, in the absence of government incentives, a free market will not provide adequate and socially beneficial primary education. Similarly, when a firm that manufactures chemicals pollutes the environment by releasing industrial waste, the social cost of producing the chemicals is higher than the private cost to the firm. That is, the private production activity of the firm creates a negative externality on society in terms of increased pollution. Therefore, to reduce the pollution, the government may impose a tax on the production of chemicals. With taxes in place, the firm will produce a socially optimal (lower) quantity of chemicals, or employ environment-friendly production processes, and thereby, lower the level of pollution. High taxes on liquor and tobacco also demonstrate the government's efforts to curtail consumption as it perceives a significant negative externality on society. The government taxes mentioned above—for protecting the environment and for curtailing the consumption of liquor and the use of tobacco—are popularly termed 'green' taxes and 'sin' taxes, respectively!

We mentioned in the beginning that the government undertakes policies to control inflation and unemployment. In a broader sense, these policies can also be interpreted as measures for reducing negative externalities: inflation and unemployment lead to lower real incomes for households and make fewer goods and services available to them. The distribution of income can become more unequal. Moreover, a lower standard of living and joblessness have the potential to create social unrest and increase the crime rate! Therefore, government must intervene. An elaborate discussion of a few other building blocks is required to understand government policies for controlling inflation and unemployment. We will take up this discussion in Part II of this book.

## IN CONCLUSION

The existence of pure public goods, natural monopolies, and externalities are clear cases of market failures. In such situations, the private sector either cannot provide goods and services profitably, or provides them with a disregard of social costs and social benefits. Therefore, the government has legitimate reasons both for undertaking the economic activities and for intervening in their functioning. Among others, these goods and services include defence, postal services, water supply, utilities, education, and conservation of the environment. Except for such cases of market failure, the private sector—through the institution of free markets—attains efficient levels of production and consumption in most other goods and services. It is for this reason that economist John Bates Clark observed—as quoted at the beginning of the chapter—that market failures are perversions of the natural economic system; we remove these perversions and keep the system. The continuing process of disinvestment of PSUs has to be judged in this context. Over the decades, in its zeal to cure the perversions of the free market economy, the government has ventured in far too many economic activities which were not real cases of market failure. Is time ticking for HMT watches?

## REFERENCES:

Coase, R., (1974), 'The Lighthouse in Economics', *Journal of Law and Economics* 17 (2): 357–376

Harrington, J. Jr., Vernon, J., and Viscusi, W., (2005), 'Introduction to Economic Regulation', *Economics of Regulation and Antitrust,* Ch. 10, pp. 357–62; 375–83, Cambridge: MIT Press

Press Information Bureau (PIB), Government of India, notes dated October 2002, January 2003 and February 2004

*The Economic Times*, "Air India on revival mode, looks to wipe-off losses in six years," April 22, 2012, http://articles. economictimes.indiatimes.com/2012-04-22/news/31382498_1_ equity-infusion-turnaround-plan-debt-ridden-carrier

# READY RECKONER

**Club Good:** A good or a service that is characterized by excludability and non-rivalry in consumption.

**Externality:** A situation in an economic activity where there is a divergence of private benefit (cost) and social benefit (cost).

**Natural Monopoly:** A situation where the per-unit cost of producing a good or a service for a given market is lower for a single firm than it would be if there were two or more firms.

**Non-excludability:** A market characteristic where a producer cannot prevent an individual—physically or by demanding an appropriate price—from consuming a good or a service.

**Non-rivalry in consumption:** A market characteristic where the consumption of a good or a service by an individual does not affect consumption by another individual.

**(Pure) Public Good:** A good or a service characterized by non-excludability and non-rivalry in consumption.

# CHAPTER 2

# BUDGET, DEFICITS, AND TAXATION

*'The state collects tax for the greater welfare of its citizens in the same way as the sun evaporates water only to return it manifold in the form of rain.' (Ch. 1.18)*

—KALIDAS, *RAGHUVANSHA*, CIRCA 4 CE

## ORIGIN OF THE BUDGET

In the last chapter, we discussed the role which the government plays in several economic activities. The scope of the government is quite broad—from establishing and running the judiciary and law and order, through undertaking activities where markets fail due to public goods and natural monopolies, to interference in activities that involve externalities and policy measures. The government needs finance to support all these economic activities. Good housekeeping, whether at the household level or at the governmental level, requires one to maintain and present a statement of the expenditures and revenues for the year gone by, and to draw up an estimate

## Presenting the *Bougette*!

Circa 1760, the Chancellor of the Exchequer in England would carry the statement of government finances to the House of Commons in a leather bag. The French word for such a leather bag is *bougette*, which became budget in English. Thus, the Chancellor would present the 'budget' in the House of Commons.

Since then, the leather bag has come to represent the annual budget of the government. Three kinds of events generate a lot of debate and discussions in India—elections, cricket, and the Union budget! Traditionally, with the substantial intervention by the Indian government in the functioning of the economy and the frequent changes that it introduced in its regulation, the economic implications of budget announcements have been critical for both Indian consumers and producers. It is no wonder then that the budget used to generate much hype and curiosity in the past. Today, however, the Union budget continues to draw a lot of attention in the news and media, but for a different reason. With the Indian economy getting increasingly integrated with rest of the world and the government steadily introducing one economic reform after the other, people are anxious to know which spheres of economic activity are getting unshackled from the government control and how would it affect their future prospects. Therefore, the finance minister is often captured on camera holding the budget bag as if he were a magician about to pull a rabbit out of his hat.

for the new year. The preparation of such an expenditure and revenue statement by the government took a formal shape in England by the middle of the eighteenth century, and used to be presented by the Chancellor of the Exchequer in the House of Commons. In India, it is the finance minister who presents the Union budget in Parliament on the last working day of February.

Every year, a few days before and after the budget, there is a flurry of news articles and discussions in newspapers and the electronic media. The budget gets discussed as if it were a cricket World Cup final. Many economic terms which, of course, we are supposed to know, are thrown at us by the experts. What we are going to attempt to do here is answer the simple queries and some pertinent questions which, somehow, maybe due to lack of time, never get clarified. Essentially, we will try to explain in brief and help you understand the process followed by the government for preparing the budget; the size of the budget; how the budget expenditure is financed; whether budget deficits are bad for the country; and what there is in the budget that one should be aware of. We take up these issues below.

## TIMING, PROCESS, AND SIZE

While the Indian government, for all its civil and administrative purposes, follows the Gregorian calendar that begins on January 1, it mandates a different twelve-month period called the fiscal year for taxation, budget, and financial reporting by the private sector. The fiscal year begins on April 1 and ends on March 31. The government has to operationalize the budget from April 1. However, before that happens, it has to get the budget approved by Parliament. This entails discussion in the Lok Sabha and the Rajya Sabha, for which the government has to allot sufficient time. And, therefore, the finance minister presents the budget on the last working day of February. Although the railway budget is presented separately, the consolidated two amounts do form part of the general budget presented by the finance minister, whose speech in Parliament consists of two parts. In Part A, the minister presents the Economic Survey of the fiscal year gone by. This is the ministry's view on the annual economic development of the country and it forms the backdrop for the presentation of the budget for new fiscal year in Part B of the speech. One can access the Economic Survey and the Budget documents at the Government of India's website at http://indiabudget.nic.in.

Along with the other items presented in the budget document, the finance minister submits the Annual Financial Statement which consists of estimated receipts and spending, which are operated through three separate accounts: (i) the Consolidated Fund, (ii) the Contingency Fund, and (iii) the Public Account. All revenues and loans raised and recovered form part of the Consolidated Fund, of which no amount can be spent without the approval of Parliament. The Contingency Fund is an imprest that is available to the president of India to meet unforeseen expenditures, such as, expenditure to tackle natural disasters or accidents. Post-facto approval of such expenditure is sought from Parliament, and an equivalent amount is drawn from the Consolidated Fund. The current corpus of this Contingency Fund is Rs 500 crore. And then, there is the Public Account which holds amounts which are held by the government in trust. These include items such as the Employees' Provident Fund and the Small Savings Collections. The funds in these items do not belong to the government, and have to be eventually returned to the people who have deposited them. No parliamentary approval is needed for such payments, except when the amounts are withdrawn from the Consolidated Fund and kept in the Public Account for specific expenditures (for example, road construction).

What is the size of the budget? One can address this issue in absolute terms as well as in relation to the nation's income. If one looks at the absolute numbers, the total budget expenditure of the Union government for the fiscal year 2010–11 was just over Rs 1100 thousand crores or about $246 billion. If we measure the size of the budget in terms of tax and non-tax revenue receipts generated by the government, this amounts to just over Rs 682 thousand crores or about $152 billion. One might be led to wonder whether this size is large or small compared to the size of the economy. One popular and useful measure of the size of an economy is called Gross Domestic Product (GDP). When we express the size of the budget as a percentage of the size of the economy, that tells us how big or small government participation is in the economy. For the fiscal year 2010–11, the total budget expenditure and the tax, non-tax, and other revenue receipts accounted for about 14 percent and 9.5 percent of India's GDP, respectively. How does this relative size of the budget compare to the relative budget size of other countries? It turns out that India's relative size of the budget and, hence, the size of government participation in the economy, is rather small compared to the relative size in other countries. For example, as reported in the World Development Report 1998–99, the tax revenue expressed as a percentage of GDP for India (the Central government), was about 10 percent, while for other countries, such as, France and the UK, it was about 39 percent and 34 percent, respectively. The relative size is quite high even for other comparable countries, such as, Brazil (20 percent) and Russia (17 percent).

## EXPENDITURE, REVENUE, AND DEFICIT
### Types of Expenditure and Revenue

In the last chapter, we identified the various reasons why the government undertakes certain activities and intervenes in the market. All the expenditures incurred on the functioning of the judiciary, maintaining law and order, routine administration, salaries, subsidies, pensions for the administrative staff, and payments on past debts are classified as revenue expenditures. Essentially, these are expenditures that do not lead to the creation of assets and are used up for the normal functioning of the government. Capital expenditures, on the other hand, include asset-creating expenditures for providing public goods, such as, dams, bridges and roads, and plants and machineries built for use in the government sector. If government expenditure forms one side of the Union budget, government receipts form the other. Government receipts are also classified into revenue receipts and capital receipts. Revenue receipts include tax receipts and non-tax receipts, such as, stamp duties, fees, and dividends, if any, from Public Sector Undertakings (PSUs). Capital receipts, on the other hand, include grants received and loans recovered by the government, and occasional disinvestment proceeds earned by selling PSUs. These are called non-debt capital receipts.

However, despite the collection of revenue receipts and non-debt capital receipts, the government may still fall short of financing for all its expenditures. In fact, lower tax and non-tax revenue receipts as a percentage of GDP does not really mean that government interference in the economy is low. It could mean that the government is inefficient in collecting sufficient revenue in relation to its expenditures. As pointed out earlier, the Union government expenditure in the fiscal year 2010–11 was higher than the tax and the non-tax revenue receipts by over Rs 400 thousand crores. Generally, the non-debt capital receipts are low, and this means that the government has to borrow to cover the deficit amount. Therefore, borrowing is a capital receipt, albeit a debt-creating capital receipt. The government has three choices for generating debt capital receipts: borrowing domestically from the public; borrowing from external financial institutions; or, under extreme conditions, borrowing from the central bank of the country. These

## GDP and GDP Growth Rate

The economic jargon that one reads in newspapers or hears on TV news and discussions, often includes terms such as GDP and GDP Growth Rate. Just as the economic well-being of a family is reflected in the total family income, economists measure the economic well-being of a nation by calculating its GDP. GDP at market prices is defined as the value of final goods and services at current market prices produced in a given period (generally one year) within the territorial boundaries of a country. Since GDP is calculated at current market prices, it is also referred to as the Nominal GDP. For example, the current market value of TVs produced within the territory of India forms part of the Nominal GDP, but the value of TVs that are manufactured abroad and imported does not. The adjective 'gross' is used, because durable assets get depreciated and the depreciated value is not subtracted from GDP. If it is, it is called the Net Domestic Product. The definition uses the adjective 'final' for goods and services. This implies that one avoids double counting. The value of the book that you are reading includes the cost of paper, ink, binding material, and the services of the author and the publisher. Thus, in calculating GDP, the value of the book will be included but not the value of all the intermediate products or services.

The Nominal GDP figures for 2010–11 and 2009–10 were about Rs 79 trillion and Rs 66 trillion, respectively. This amounts to about 20 percent growth in the Nominal GDP. Does the entire change reflect a 'real' increase in GDP? Not really, for both prices and production may have increased over the year. If the production of goods and services had not increased during the year, then the entire 20 percent growth rate would be attributed to an increase in prices alone. And this does not reflect any 'real' increase in the production of goods and services. Therefore, whenever the GDP growth rate is reported, it corresponds to the growth rate in real GDP. A detailed discussion on this topic will be covered in later chapter when we discuss the phenomenon called inflation.

three forms of borrowing are undertaken by selling new government securities or bonds.

## Types of Deficit

Based on the types of budget expenditures and revenues as defined above, economists consider three kinds of deficits for measuring the prudent handling of government finances. The first is the Revenue Deficit, which measures the difference between revenue expenditure and revenue receipts. A deficit of this kind shows the management of government finances in a poor light, for it shows that the government has to borrow money to finance administrative activities which do not lead to the creation of any assets. This is akin to a household that needs to borrow funds to pay for the services of housemaids, a driver, and a gardener! Of course, if a household borrows to invest in a child's higher education, this borrowing is for an expenditure which will create an asset in the form of human capital, and such borrowing will always be preferred to the former.

The second type of deficit is the Fiscal Deficit, which refers to the difference between the government's total expenditure and the total non-debt receipts. In short, this indicates that the government has exhausted all options for financing its expenditure, and the only recourse left is to borrow. Thus, Fiscal Deficit shows the total debt generated by the government to finance the total budget expenditure. Such a deficit is justified as long as the expenditures are being incurred to finance activities leading to the creation of national assets. High fiscal deficits become a matter of worry, for, if incurred year after year, they cumulatively create a huge debt for the government. The recent experience of Greece and a few other European countries shows that cumulative high fiscal deficits can lead countries to bankruptcy of the governments.

Yet another deficit that is considered by an incumbent government is the Primary Deficit. This deficit is defined as the difference between the Fiscal Deficit and the interest payment on debts incurred in earlier years. If one removes the interest payments from the Fiscal Deficit, the Primary Deficit becomes a smaller number. The incumbent government uses this statistic to show that the interest payments on the previous debt are not of its making. When this component is removed from the Fiscal Deficit and the resultant deficit turns out to be very small, it proves the prudent management of the budget by the incumbent government.

## Size and Composition of Deficits

Table 2.1 shows the trends in Central government deficits expressed as a percentage of GDP over a number of years. The Fiscal Responsibility and Budget Management Act (FRBM) of 2003 had mandated that the Central government's Fiscal Deficit and Revenue Deficit as a percentage of GDP must come down to 3 percent and 0 percent, respectively, by 2008–09. The trend up to 2007–08 clearly showed that the Central government did a good job and considerably reduced the deficits. In fact, the Fiscal Deficit was brought down to below 3 percent in 2007–08, and the Revenue Deficit was only about 41 percent of the Fiscal Deficit. This shows that relatively higher amounts were being spent on asset-creating expenditures.

However, the world was hit by a global recession at that time and India was no exception to it. To avoid the recession, the government had to engage in an expansionary fiscal policy which, once again, contributed to an increased percentage of the Fiscal and the Revenue Deficits in the years 2008–09 and 2009–10. While we will discuss expansionary fiscal policy in a later chapter, it will suffice at this time to say that it involves increasing government expenditure and/ or reducing taxes to reduce unemployment. An expansionary fiscal policy has to be temporary in nature and it is desirable that the deficits decrease eventually. In this context, the Thirteenth Finance Commission, under the chairpersonship of Dr Vijay Kelkar, recommended a revised date of 2013–14 by

**Table 2.1: Fiscal, Revenue, and Primary Deficits of the Central Government (% of GDP)**

| Deficit | 2005–06 | 2006–07 | 2007–08 | 2008–09 | 2009–10 | 2010–11 |
|---|---|---|---|---|---|---|
| Fiscal | 4.0 | 3.3 | 2.5 | 6.0 | 6.3 | 4.8 |
| Revenue | 2.5 | 1.9 | 1.1 | 4.5 | 5.1 | 3.5 |
| Primary | 0.4 | –0.2 | –0.9 | 2.6 | 3.1 | 1.7 |
| (Revenue/Fiscal)x100 | 63.0 | 56.3 | 41.4 | 75.2 | 80.7 | 72.5 |

Source: *Economic Survey*, 2010–11

the end of which the Fiscal and the Revenue Deficits should be brought down to 3 percent and 0 percent respectively. However, the prospect of this happening is low, for Indian economy has not fully recovered from recession even in 2012. In fact, the International Monetary Fund has all along been recommending that the Fiscal Deficit should not be more than 3 percent of GDP. Notice also the last row in Table 2.1. The Revenue Deficit as a percentage of the Fiscal Deficit has been extremely high in the recent past, averaging about 75 percent. Such a high percentage is worrisome, for it tells us that most of the debt that the government is incurring is being used for routine administrative expenses and will not lead to any asset creation.

The deficits of only the Central government are reported above. Bigger deficits emerge when the deficits of state governments are included. For example, the combined Fiscal, Revenue, and Primary Deficits of the Central and the state governments for the year 2009–10 were 9.59 percent, 5.06

percent and 4.29 percent of India's GDP. Why do economists not look favourably upon a high Fiscal Deficit (even if the Revenue Deficit is low)? To give a simple household analogy: one must cut one's coat according to the size of the cloth! However, this argument does not go very far if one argues that the government is justified in borrowing to finance asset-creating expenditures on dams, roads, education. The reason why a high Fiscal Deficit is discouraged lies in its linkage to interest rates, private investments, and foreign trade deficit. Let us try to understand this linkage.

When the government's Fiscal Deficit is large, it implies that the government has to borrow heavily. This means that the demand for loans will rise in the market, causing interest rates to go up. As interest rates rise, the cost of borrowing for private firms goes up. As the cost of borrowing rises, firms find that fewer and fewer investment projects are economically viable. Therefore, private firms borrow less and do not invest in new projects. In fact, they get out of some of the existing investment projects, for loans are costly. The fall in private investments naturally has an adverse impact on employment generation and income. In economics, this phenomenon is called the 'Crowding Out' of private investments by public borrowing. There is one more reason why a heavy Fiscal Deficit may have additional adverse effects. *Ceteris Paribus*, that is, other things remaining the same, as the government borrows more and more from the credit market, it may even have to borrow from foreign sources. It goes without saying that, since the interest rates are high, foreign firms and institutions sense profit opportunities and are happy to supply funds from abroad. As foreign funds start flowing into the country, foreign firms and institutions have to exchange their currency with the Indian rupee. This means that the demand for the Indian rupee goes up and it appreciates. That is, if the exchange rate, initially, was one US dollar to Rs 50, due to the additional demand for rupees by foreigners, the new exchange rate would become, say, one US dollar to Rs 40.[1] When the rupee appreciates in this manner, one US dollar fetches fewer rupees and, therefore, Indian exports become expensive and imports become cheaper. This results in lower exports and higher imports for India, leading to a higher trade deficit for the country. Thus, a high Fiscal Deficit may lead to a very high trade deficit.

Of course, one must also remember that accumulation of fiscal deficits over time leads to large public debt, both domestic and foreign. PIIGS (Portugal, Italy, Ireland, Greece, and Spain) countries in Europe have found themselves in very critical condition on this issue in the recent past. For example, Greece's debt had crossed more than 142 percent of its GDP in 2010, and importantly, she was unable to repay the debt and interest payments, leading to disastrous consequences for its economy.

---

1   Of course, the Indian rupee is sliding against the US dollar for quite some time despite high interest rates. High interest rates attract foreign funds, however, only if an important caveat of *ceteris paribus* is met. If the social, economic, and political environment is not congenial, foreign funds would not come despite high interest rates. With policy paralysis on major economic fronts, foreigners would be hesitant to invest in or import goods from India. In fact, Indians themselves may take their investments abroad. In such a case, Indian rupee may depreciate despite high interest rates and trade deficit will continue to be high.

# TAXATION AND FISCAL CONSOLIDATION
## *Principles of Taxation*

If governments wish to avoid budget deficits or, at least, minimize them, it is clear that they have no other option but to tax their people and firms. Therefore, although taxes are highly unpopular, they become a regrettable necessity for financing the business of the government. And this begs the questions: Which principle should guide a government to collect taxes from society? Unfortunately, there is no one single philosophical principle on which governments can rely. First, there is the Benefit Principle which holds that people and firms must be taxed in proportion to the benefits they receive from the government. That is, if A uses a toll road five times more than B, then A must pay a toll which is five times the toll paid by B. Second, the Ability to Pay Principle holds that the taxes which people pay should relate to their income and wealth; that is, if A has a higher income than B, A should pay higher taxes than B, because A's ability to earn and, therefore, pay, is more. Third, the Horizontal Equity and the Vertical Equity Principles state that those who are equal should be taxed equally, and those who are unequal must be taxed unequally. That is, if A and B have the same income, they should pay the same tax, but if A has a higher income than B, then A should pay more tax than B. These Equity principles essentially focus on the issue of fairness. Finally, yet another principle that is considered is the Principle of Economic Efficiency. It states that taxes should have a minimal effect on free market consumption and production decisions.

37

So, which principle is used by governments and which practices are followed? In reality, most governments make pragmatic compromises in taxation and apply a combination of principles. Charging toll for an expressway, charging cess for water, and the collection of taxes from residents so that the local government can build paved roads, are examples of the use of the Benefit Principle. It is understood that the higher the income or wealth, the higher are the taxes collected by the government. This reflects the use of the Ability to Pay Principle. The Equity (Horizontal) Principle can be consistent with both the Benefit Principle and the Ability to Pay Principle—when two individuals receive the same service from the use of an expressway they pay the same tax (toll). Similarly, if two individuals have an equal income, they pay equal taxes. On the other hand, the efficiency principle may be at odds with the equity principle. For example, consider essential commodities, such as, food. The demand for food is highly insensitive to price changes, for one cannot live without food. Therefore, taxes charged on essential commodities, such as food, may increase food prices but it will have little effect on consumption. Here, the tax is 'efficient' in the sense that after-tax consumption is not much different from what it would have been before the imposition of tax. However, such tax on food does not maintain vertical equity, for both the rich and the poor would consume more or less the same amount of food and pay the same amount of tax, although their incomes would be quite different. Therefore, two individuals with unequal income are not being treated unequally!

## *Types of Taxes*

All taxes are classified as either Direct Taxes or Indirect Taxes. Direct taxes, such as, personal income tax, corporate tax and wealth tax, are charged directly on people and firms. Taxes like income tax are consistent with the Ability to Pay Principle. For example, in Proportional income tax, all taxpayers pay exactly the same proportion of their income as tax. Of course, needless to say, the absolute amount of tax is higher for a higher income. Income tax is generally made even more redistributive by making it Progressive, in that, a higher-income individual not only pays a higher amount as tax but also pays a higher proportion of income as tax. A Regressive income tax, on the other hand, takes a higher proportion of income in taxes from a poor individual than it does from a rich individual.

Indirect taxes are taxes that are charged on goods and services and, therefore, are charged indirectly on people or firms. These taxes include Excise Duty charged on the production of goods; Sales Tax imposed on goods at the time of sale; Octroi charged on goods entering a city; Service Tax imposed on services; Property Tax on real estate; and Customs Duty on the import of goods. Indirect taxes are easier to levy and collect since they can be charged at the point of sale, both at the retail and the wholesale level. However, indirect taxes turn out to be Regressive, for poor individuals generally end up paying a larger proportion of their income as indirect taxes than the rich individual.

## Composition of Taxes

Historically, indirect taxes have been the main source of tax revenue for the Indian government. As indicated in Table 2.2, during the fiscal year 1991–92—the year from which substantial economic reforms were undertaken in India—the proportion of indirect taxes was as high as 75 percent. Direct tax collections were low since the tax base itself was low. People's incomes were low and, due to the existence of a large informal sector, the incomes of a large section of society were not reported. It was difficult to justify a very high proportion of indirect taxes because, as pointed our earlier, indirect taxes tend to be regressive. Moreover, the differential rates of various indirect taxes on different goods distort the free-market signalling of the relative prices of goods. On the other hand, direct taxes, like income tax, do not distort the relative prices in the market. And, at the same time, they live up to the principle of the Ability to Pay. What happened then, in the couple of decades since 1991, to make the share of direct taxes become 43 percent by 2005–06 and further increase to about 57 percent in 2010–11?

One reason was that the government was concerned about the taxation issues mentioned above as well as the mounting budget deficits. In fact, if we consider the combined deficits of the Central and the state governments, in the fiscal year 2001–02, the combined revenue deficit was as high as 7.05 percent and the combined fiscal deficit was 9.86 percent. These were record-high percentages. The economists who advise the government—aware of the fact that it is difficult

### Table 2.2: Tax Revenue as a Percentage of Gross Tax Revenue*

| Tax | 1991–92 | 2005–06 | 2010–11 |
| --- | --- | --- | --- |
| Direct Taxes (including): | 22.6 | 43.0 | 56.5 |
| Personal income tax | | 15.3 | 16.1 |
| Corporate income tax | | 27.7 | 40.4 |
| Indirect Taxes (including): | 74.8 | 54.5 | 42.2 |
| Customs | | 17.8 | 15.4 |
| Excise | | 30.4 | 17.7 |
| Service | | 6.3 | 9.1 |

* Source: *Economic Survey*, 2010–11

to curtail government expenditures once the government is committed to them—recommended a substantial enhancing of the revenue collection, thereby reducing the deficits. This effort has been popularly known as revenue-led fiscal consolidation. To this end, therefore, a concerted effort was made to rationalize the tax system, make it fair and efficient, and enable it to generate more tax revenue, keeping in mind that very high income tax rates have a negative impact on the incentive to work. Today, the marginal personal income tax rate, that is, the progressive income tax rate applicable to the highest personal income tax bracket is 30 percent, which is about the same as that in the US. This is a far cry from the highest bracket marginal income tax rate of 97.75 percent that existed in India in 1974–75. The government has also striven to expand the tax base by making it mandatory for citizens to have an income tax Permanent Account Number (PAN). Moreover, the recent Direct Tax Code bill introduced in Parliament in 2010 has proposed bringing the corporate income tax rate to just 30 percent.

There have been similar reforms in the indirect tax system as well. Indirect taxes were being levied at different stages of production and sale, whereby, at every stage, an additional tax was getting levied on the total value of the good. Moreover, a tax was also getting levied on the taxes paid at the earlier stage of production. This phenomenon is called cascading of taxes. To avoid a multiplicity of taxation and cascading, both the Central and the state governments introduced Value Added Tax (VAT). VAT, charged by the state governments, is now levied only on the value addition made by a particular firm or enterprise, where value addition refers to the total sales proceeds of a firm minus the cost of the material inputs used. For example, if the sales proceeds of an apparel manufacturing firm are Rs 1 million, and the cost of materials consumed, such as, textile, leather, buttons, and electricity, is Rs 600,000, then VAT will be applied only on Rs 400,000, not on Rs 1 million. Similarly, the Central government uses Central Value Added Tax (CENVAT) to charge central excise duties. As indicated elsewhere, excise duty is the duty charged at the production stage of a good. Here, too, tax will be charged on the value addition, that is, on the value of production net of the material cost. To take these reforms further—as proposed in the Thirteenth Finance Commission Report (2010)—the government is committed to integrating all the indirect taxes and introducing a single value added tax which will be called Goods and Services

## The Laffer Curve: On Which Side of the Hump Are You?

Professor Arthur Laffer was a member of the economic policy advisory board for US President Ronald Reagan during 1981–89. He also advised Prime Minister Margaret Thatcher of UK on fiscal policy matters. The story goes that, sitting in a restaurant in Washington, D.C., Professor Laffer drew an inverted U-shaped curve on a paper napkin to explain the relation between tax revenue and tax rate. His essential idea was that, if the marginal tax rate is very high, a reduction in the tax rate would actually increase tax revenue. The logic of the argument is explained as follows:

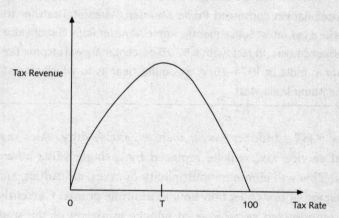

If a government does not levy tax, that is, the tax rate is zero, there will be no tax revenue. As the tax rate increases, so will the tax revenue until the tax rate reaches an optimal level T. If the tax rate rises above T, the tax revenue will begin to fall.

Of course, at 100 percent tax rate, the tax revenue would be zero since it would completely discourage all economic activity. One does not really know the exact shape of the Laffer Curve for different taxes and different countries. However, the idea is that, after the level of optimal tax rate T, any increase in the tax rate would lead to a substantive disincentive to work, and the resultant fall in GDP would lower the tax revenue. High tax rates may also lead to tax evasion which is illegal. Thus, whether or not tax revenue will increase or decrease when the tax rate is changed depends upon which side of the hump the original tax rate is.

President Ronald Reagan reduced tax rates and the same paper napkin convinced Prime Minister Margaret Thatcher to reduce tax rates. Subsequently, Prime Minister Rajiv Gandhi also reduced taxes. In fact, with a 97.75 percent marginal income tax rate in India in 1974–75, it was quite clear as to which side of the hump India was!

Tax (GST). Indirect taxes, such as, excise duty, sales tax, and service tax, will be replaced by a single value added tax. This will eliminate multiplicity of taxes, cascading, and wastage of tax-collection time at multiple points. Currently, an empowered committee of finance ministers of the state governments and of the Central government is working on the modalities of implementation of tax, tax rate, and the formula to divide the tax proceeds between the Centre and the state governments. It is expected that GST will be introduced earliest by the end of 2012 or in 2013.

Further, since 1994, the government has been gradually introducing service tax as well. Today, services, ranging from accounting to xeroxing and banking to tourism, account for about 60 percent of India's GDP. All these services are an economic activity just like the production and sale of goods. Therefore, it was absurd that services were not taxed earlier. Currently, about 117 services are being taxed and the number will only grow over time. As shown in Table 2.2, about 9 percent of the gross tax revenue of the Central government comes from services. On the foreign trade front, India used to levy very high customs duties, that is, duties on imported products. Until 1990–91, India followed highly trade-restrictive policies, with import restrictions and high customs duties—the obvious way to protect domestic firms from foreign competition. But this has changed since the onset of import liberalization starting 1990–91. The process of liberalization was also speeded up with the formation of the World Trade Organization (WTO) in 1995. As a result, today, the peak customs duty has come down to 10 percent. A little later, in a separate chapter, we will take up the issues related to WTO and trade liberalization.

## TAKEAWAYS ON THE BUDGET

What are the takeaways of the preceding discussion? Perhaps one cannot match the poetic expression for government expenses and taxation as enunciated by Kalidasa in the classical play, *Raghuvansha*. Moreover, centuries have passed and one cannot afford to maintain the same level of innocence that Kalidasa may have had in understanding fiscal matters. The preceding discussion on matters of government expenses, taxation, and deficits may alert one to watch the Union budget speech by the finance minister on the last working day of February. And, one may just read and/or watch the budget news and discussions out of both popular and academic interest. When a budget is presented and approved in Parliament, it is we the people who are doing it through our elected representatives. In this context, the reporting by the media about the pre-budget interactions that the government has with various stakeholders, such as, industry associations and consumer groups, may hold our attention. Such interactions may give us a clue or two about what issues will be dealt with in the ensuing budget.

For example, we know that more and more services are being taxed now. In fact, in the latest Union budget presented on March 2012, the Government of India has proposed a negative list approach to extending the scope of service tax. That is, it is proposed that all services will be taxed at 12 percent henceforth except the ones that are mentioned in the negative list. This negative list includes only 17 service areas that are exempted from service tax. For example, these include government administrative services, high school and university education, agricultural services, public transport, entry to amusement parks, some government approved vocational courses, rent on residential dwellings, and a few other. Going by the negative list, your landlord will charge service tax on the rented premise you use for office space, however, he or she cannot charge service tax on the rented apartment you use for residential purpose. Today, the marginal personal income tax has come down to 30 percent, and one should not expect any further lowering of this tax. However, if one has some spare savings to park profitably, one may want to keep a watch on whether or not there are any additions to or deletions from tax-deductible financial investments. While some of the provisions of the budget are of tactical importance to individuals for managing their personal finances, other affect us on a broader, societal level. For example, if the revenue deficit expressed as a percentage of the fiscal deficit continues to be very high, it is an indication to you that most of the government borrowings are being used for administrative or similar expenses which do not lead to asset-creation. If the fiscal deficit is quite high as compared to the rule of thumb of 3 percent of GDP on a sustained basis, it should be a matter of alarm. For, such a high deficit would eventually lead to high interest rates which would crowd out private investments, and may lead to a worsening trade deficit for the country. And, in a participatory democracy, it is possible to raise such concerns with the elected representatives.

So, the next time you tune in to the budget presentation, here is a draft checklist of questions for which you may seek answers:

1. How much is the projected Fiscal and Revenue Deficit? Is the government moving towards the prudent norms of 3 percent and 0 percent, respectively?

2. How much is the Revenue Deficit as a percentage of the Fiscal Deficit? That is to say, 'Is the deficit spending going into asset-creation or is it simply for administrative purposes?'

3. How much is India's GDP and what is the projected GDP growth rate? A better growth rate of, say, 8 percent or more, is an indicator of a positive environment for your business growth as well.

4. Has the marginal corporate income tax rate been brought down?

5. Have the personal income tax slabs been raised for standard deductions?

6. Which additional services are being removed from the negative list and come under the service tax regime? For example, 'Are second-class train fares, the amusement park tickets or renting of tractors being brought under the tax regime?'

7. Excise duty and service tax rates were lowered a few years ago to combat recession. Now that the GDP growth rate looks somewhat promising, will there be a continued upward revision in these rates?

8. Is the GST finally getting implemented from the coming financial year?

9. Is there any further reduction in customs duties on imports that are of interest to my business?

10. Is the government going to allow Foreign Direct Investment (FDI) in multi-brand retailing that may give competition to my grocery business?

The budget is an annual, one-time phenomenon or event which affects our economic life and decisions. However, there are two other institutional set-ups that are not one-time phenomena, form part of our economic life, and with which we engage intermittently—the banking system and the stock market. We turn to these two in the next chapter.

## REFERENCES:

GOI, 'Union Budget and Economic Survey', http:/ indiabudget. nic.in/, site developed by National Informatics Centre and information provided by Ministry of Finance, Government of India (GOI)

GUK, 'History of the Budget, HM Treasury, Govt. of UK', http:// www.hm-treasury.gov.uk/about_budget.htm, Government of UK (GUK)

# READY RECKONER

**Ability to Pay Principle:** The taxes which people pay should relate to their earning capacity, income and wealth.

**Benefit Principle:** Individuals and firms must be taxed in proportion to the benefits they receive from the government.

**Capital Expenditure:** Asset-creating expenditure on providing public goods, such as, dams, bridges and roads, and plants and machineries built for use in the government sector.

**Capital Receipt:** The debt receipt, which includes domestic borrowings from the public, external borrowings, and occasional borrowing from the central bank of the country. And the non-debt receipt which comprises net grants received by the government, loan recoveries, and disinvestment proceeds earned by selling PSUs.

**Direct Tax:** Taxes charged directly on individuals and firms.

**Fiscal Deficit:** The difference between the government's total expenditure and the total non-debt receipts.

**GDP:** The Gross Domestic Product (GDP) at market prices, defined as the value of final goods and services at current market prices produced in a given period (generally one year) within the territorial boundaries of a country. Also referred to as the Nominal GDP.

**Horizontal Equity:** Those who are equal should be taxed equally.

**Indirect Tax:** Taxes that are charged on goods and services and, therefore, are charged indirectly on individuals and firms.

**Laffer Curve:** An inverted U-shaped graphic relation between tax revenue (on the y-axis) and tax rate (on the x-axis) attributed to Professor Arthur Laffer.

**Primary Deficit:** The difference between Fiscal Deficit and the interest on the previous government's debt.

**Progressive Income Tax:** Income tax where a higher income attracts a higher proportion of income tax.

**Proportional Income Tax:** Income tax where all taxpayers pay exactly the same proportion of their income as tax.

**Regressive Income Tax:** Income tax where a higher income attracts a lower proportion of income tax.

**Revenue Deficit:** The difference between revenue expenditure and revenue receipts.

**Revenue Expenditure:** Expenditure incurred on the functioning of the judiciary, maintaining law and order, routine administration, salaries, subsidies, pensions for administrative staff, and payments on past debts.

**Revenue Receipt:** Receipt from taxes and non-tax receipts, such as, stamp duty, fees, and dividends, if any, from PSUs.

**Value Added Tax:** Tax levied on the difference between sales proceeds and material cost. Essentially, it is a tax on the factor income generated in an economic activity.

**Vertical Equity:** Those who are unequal must be taxed unequally.

# CHAPTER 3

# MONEY, BANKING, AND
# THE STOCK MARKET

*'It is a wise man who lives with money in the bank, it is a
fool who dies that way.'*

—AN OLD FRENCH PROVERB

## BACKGROUND

We are aware, via periodic flashy news and discussions every
February, that the Union budget is associated with the finances
of the Central government and directly affects our economic
lives. Besides this, there are two other financial institutions
which are intricately linked to our financial lives—the banking
system and the stock market. Banks are silent but salient
partners in holding and channelling our private finances but
seem to make news only on rare occasions when a bank is
liquidated or when it runs out of cash to honour withdrawal
demands by its customers. Similarly, the stock market is an

important partner in directing our finances to firms and is frequently a part of the news hour specials. In this chapter, we will endeavour to understand more about these institutions. By the end of it, we will be in a position to understand the abstract concept called 'money' as against the common English usage of the term; we will understand how paper currency evolved, how banks create 'money' in the economy, and how changes in the share prices on the stock market reflect the changing perception of the market regarding the profitability of private firms.

## WHAT IS MONEY?

In common English parlance, the word 'money' is a catch-all used to describe salary, profit, rent, interest earned, income, savings and wealth. In economics, however, money is defined in a very peculiar fashion. Salary, profit, rent, interest earned are all sources of income for individuals or firms. This income is measured per unit of time. For example, a salary is earned per month and the profit made is reported for a given financial year. Even the GDP of a nation is expressed for a given period, say, a year. On the other hand, wealth is a stock concept, which is the result of accumulation of savings over time. Therefore, it is quoted at a given point in time and not for a given period of time. For example, when the media reports that Azim Premji is the richest man in India, what is really meant is that his savings accumulated over time were the highest at that particular point in time. Thus, the adjective 'richest' refers to a stock concept. Finally, money as understood in economics, or money supply as defined by the central bank, is yet another concept. Understanding this concept is useful and will shed light on the monetary policy of the central bank which we will discuss in later chapters. Let us consider some examples to understand the concept of 'money'.

If a tourist were to ask, 'How far is the Gateway of India from Mumbai airport?' one might answer, 'About sixteen kilometres' or 'About an hour away.' These answers are expressed in a standard unit of measurement of distance called kilometre and a standard unit of measurement of time called hour. Similarly, when we talked about the Union budget, expenditures, deficits, GDP, and taxes in the previous chapter, we expressed these magnitudes in terms of money, that is, Indian rupees or US dollars. Thus, money is a standard unit of measurement for economic magnitudes just as a kilometre and an hour are for distance and time, respectively.

However, money is much more than just a standard unit of measurement. It also represents the cash balance that a household has on an average during a given period. Consider the following exclamation one may hear in a household: 'I withdrew Rs 10,000 just a week ago from the ATM and now you want me to withdraw another Rs 8,000 today?' At the heart of this exclamation is the practical issue of how much and how often a family may need to withdraw cash from an automated teller machine (ATM). The issue involves competing arguments—family members may not want to keep their hard-earned monthly salary (income) at home, for there is always the risk of theft or pilferage. The family would also lose out on interest amount by not keeping the salary in a savings bank account. Therefore, one may wish to withdraw cash only when required. However, one needs cash every now and then, entailing frequent visits to the ATM which becomes irksome. In fact, it involves wasting precious time which one would rather spend on other important activities. Thus, it would make sense for the family to keep some optimal amount at home. The necessity for holding an optimal cash balance over a given period arises because family members earn income periodically (say, monthly) by selling their labour services, but they need to spend cash on buying goods and services throughout the month. It is clear that the income and expenditure patterns are not synchronous, and holding an optimal amount of cash balance would facilitate the exchange of the family's labour services with the goods and services it wishes to buy. Therefore, holding an optimal cash balance serves an important purpose—it facilitates transactions. That is to say, the optimal cash balance functions as a medium of exchange. Money is just that—a medium of exchange. The demand for such cash balances is referred to as the 'transactions demand' for money.

In fact, some families would insist that it is advisable to keep some extra idle cash at home, since one requires a cash balance not only for regular expected expenses during the month but also for the unexpected ones. For example, one never knows when the in-laws or relatives are going to pay an unannounced visit! Thus, a household needs to hold a cash balance as a precaution against unanticipated expenses. The demand for such cash balances is referred to as the 'precautionary demand' for money. John Maynard Keynes, the father of modern macroeconomics, argued that there is yet another reason why households may like to keep cash on hand. Many people speculate in markets for shares (stock), real estate, and/or precious metals with a view to making capital gains. One would sell an asset—financial or real—when prices were high and hold the proceeds in the form of cash. When prices go down, one would once again buy the asset, hoping to sell it later when prices rise. In the process, some cash balances are held for speculative purposes.

The above discussion shows that households keep cash balances for three purposes—transactions, precautionary, and speculative. These cash balances facilitate the exchange of goods and services, including the buying (and selling) of financial or real assets. Milton Friedman, recipient of the Nobel Memorial Prize in Economic Sciences, called these cash balances the 'temporary abode of purchasing power'. Hence, apart from being a unit of measurement, money is also a medium of exchange and a temporary store of value (abode of purchasing power). Therefore, the cash balance that a household maintains is money. Moreover, one also makes payments for buying goods and services by writing cheques. These cheques are issued against the value of chequable deposits one holds with a bank. Therefore, the value of demand deposits or chequable deposits against which one can write cheques is also money. The world over, the currency with the public (that is, cash balances on hand) and the demand deposits with banks are considered money. With some variation, the central banks of almost all countries accept this definition of money as the narrow definition of money, denoted as M1.

## Money and Liquidity

It is easy to figure out why the value of shares or stocks is not included in the definition of money. Shares are not used as a medium of exchange to buy goods and services. However, one could, in principle, sell off shares and use the cash to buy a good or a service. But even then, shares cannot be sold instantly and there could be a loss of value if one tried to make a distress sale of shares for this purpose. In this sense, shares are 'illiquid' financial assets, where liquidity is defined as the ease with which a financial or a real asset can be converted into cash without much loss of value. Therefore, money—the currency with the public and the chequable demand deposits—is the most liquid financial asset. Interest-bearing time deposits or fixed deposits with banks can be considered as being liquid to some degree, for one can convert a fixed deposit into cash with a very minor penalty for cutting short the maturity period. The degree of liquidity for a time deposit is less than that for cash or a demand deposit but is higher than that for real assets and shares. Therefore, another definition called 'Broad Money'—which is popularly denoted as M3 by central banks—also includes time deposits as money. The definition of M1 and M3 and their amounts

### Table 3.1: Definition of Money*

| Definition | Components | Rupees Crore (31-3-2011) |
|---|---|---|
| Narrow | | 16,35,570 |
| Money (M1) | Currency with the public | 9,14,197 |
| | Demand deposits with banks | 7,17,660 |
| | 'Other' deposits with RBI | 3,713 |
| Broad | | 64,99,549 |
| Money (M3) | Narrow Money (M1) | 16, 35,570 |
| | Time deposits with banks | 48,63,979 |

* Source: *RBI Annual Report*, 2010–11, p. 179

are reported in Table 3.1 above. There are quite a few other definitions of money introduced by the Reserve Bank of India (RBI). However, a discussion of those is beyond the scope of this book. It should suffice to say that the definitions vary according to the liquidity of the financial assets.

## MONEY AND THE BANKING SYSTEM

The evolution of money and of the banking system around the world has an interesting beginning. Back in time—quite a few millennia ago—a person could exchange a good with another person, but only if the other person required that good, and, more importantly, had the requisite good to offer which the first person wanted. This matching of mutual demands for a barter exchange, called 'double coincidence of wants', was a difficult proposition. To give an example from the present times, let us suppose you are good at giving personal tuition in mathematics and would like your child to learn classical music. If money did not exist, you would need to find a person who was interested in giving classical music lessons to your child, and, in exchange, was ready to accept mathematics tuition for his or her child. Now, the chance of this coincidence is remote. Besides, you would have a difficult time agreeing on how many mathematics sessions—or a fraction thereof—were equal to one music session. With money, you could give mathematics tuition to the child of any person who agreed to your fees. The income you earned this way could be spent entirely, or in part, on your child's music lessons from yet another person who was prepared to teach music in return for money. Thus, money eliminates the problem of a double coincidence of wants. You can see that the evolution of money in modern times, in the form of paper currency, has made our lives immensely simpler. As pointed out in the following box, it is due to our faith in the Indian government and its central bank that we accept the paper currency issued by RBI as money.

The progression of money did not stop there. Enterprising businessmen saw another opportunity once paper currency became the norm. We have already seen that the value of demand deposits with bank is also considered money, since one can write a cheque (that is, use that amount from the bank) to make payments. But, come to think of it, why would a bank sit on idle cash, waiting to serve its customers as and when they needed the money? A bank is, after all, a profit-making entity and must earn income through some activities. They earn a profit as a consequence of three tendencies of the depositors. First, when people deposit money in a bank, generally, they do not withdraw their money immediately. That is a foregone conclusion, else, why would they deposit money in the bank to start with? Second, even if people do withdraw cash from their bank accounts sooner or later, they do not withdraw it in full. And third, people do not withdraw money simultaneously with others. A bank is cognizant of these features. Therefore, it keeps aside as reserve a certain portion of the initial cash deposit (primary deposit) of an account holder and lends the remaining amount to a firm, on condition that the firm opens an account in the bank, in which the money loaned is deposited. This creates an additional deposit—a secondary deposit—with the bank, for which no new cash was actually deposited in the bank. Once again, the bank assumes that the firm will not withdraw all the cash at one time. Hence, keeping aside a certain portion of this secondary deposit as reserve, the bank lends the remaining amount to yet another firm. This process continues, and, thereby, the bank creates chequable deposits which are much larger than the initial cash deposited by a person. This multiple creation of credit and deposit allows banks to charge interest on loans and make a profit.

Reason will tell you that the lower the cash reserve maintained by a bank against its primary and secondary deposits, the higher would be its loan and deposit expansion.

**I promise to pay the bearer the sum of one hundred rupees!**

If you were to read carefully the writing on a hundred-rupee currency note, you would find a signed promise by the governor of the RBI, stating the above caption. Isn't this promise quite meaningless? After all, the governor is promising merely to exchange a one-hundred rupee note with one hundred rupees!

And yet, the promise demonstrates the evolution of currency notes issued by the central bank of a country and proves the faith which people have in the national currency. Quite a few millennia ago, man began using a variety of things as money. These articles, used as money, were portable, countable and could be exchanged with other individuals to acquire commodities. Shells, beads, and precious stones were a few such items which were used as money. With advances in metallurgy, precious metals, such as, silver and gold began to get used as money. Kings and queens started issuing their own gold and silver coins. As the volume and value of transactions increased exponentially over time, people found it cumbersome and risky to carry valuable silver and gold wherever they went for business. Instead, they started depositing the silver and gold with goldsmiths who would give them deposit receipts. These deposit receipts were used as money, which were actually a proxy for the people's silver and gold held with the goldsmiths. Thus, private currency notes began to get issued and circulated. Governments, too, saw an opportunity in this development and started issuing their own paper currency which was backed by silver and gold. Interestingly, the currency term Rupee, used in countries, such as, India, Indonesia, Pakistan, Nepal, and Sri Lanka, is derived from the Sanskrit word for silver, *rupyaka*.

As time passed, the enormous growth in trade and commerce had to be measured in terms of currency, the supply of which was limited by the availability of silver and gold. Governments realized that, as long as people had faith in the government and its central bank, and, as long as money was used as a medium of exchange, people would not come back to the central bank to demand their silver or gold. Hence, governments discontinued the direct association between precious metals and the amount of paper currency. Today, RBI is not required to have more than Rs 115 crores in gold to back rupee currency. No wonder then, that the governor of RBI can only promise to pay hundred rupees to the bearer of a hundred-rupee note!

It would be possible, therefore, for an unscrupulous bank, motivated by greed, to set aside an extremely low proportion of its deposits as cash. This would pose a real threat to depositors, for their deposits would not be backed by sufficient cash. Moreover, if, for some reason, a large number of depositors were to withdraw cash at the same time, the bank would be unable to pay up, leading to a run on the bank. If the scare of a bank run were to spread to other banks, there is always a chance that the banking system would collapse. To prevent this, RBI sets some minimum limits on the cash reserve to be maintained by banks against their deposit liabilities. This minimum limit, enforced by RBI, is called the Cash Reserve Ratio (CRR), and it varies from 20 percent to 3 percent of the deposit liabilities of banks. Furthermore, RBI is also concerned that a disproportionate amount of loan should not be given to less creditworthy and risky borrowers. To guard against this, RBI mandates that banks maintain a certain proportion of their deposit liabilities in the form of secure investments—government securities, gold and/or cash. This RBI requirement is called the Statutory Liquidity Ratio (SLR), which was as high as 39 percent a few decades ago and currently is at 23 percent.

As mentioned in the following box, loan defaults and the consequent bank failure tend to spread panic among the deposit holders, resulting in a bank run. If the panic situation spreads, the entire banking system faces the risk of failure. Runs on the banks arise due to deposit holders' loss of faith and confidence in the banks. To counter such panic situations, governments generally support a deposit insurance mechanism for the banks. This initiative began in the aftermath of the great depression of the 1930s. Today, in India, deposit holders' bank accounts are insured up to a maximum of Rs 1 lakh each, per insured bank by the Deposit Insurance and Credit Guarantee Corporation (DICGC). For example, in the event of a bank failure, if a bank owes an individual an amount of Rs 97,000 inclusive of interest, the full amount will be paid to the deposit holder by DICGC. However, if the bank owes Rs 1,35,000, only Rs 1 lakh will be paid by DICGC.

Bank runs are less likely to occur when deposit holders are assured of the value of their money in the banks. There have been some instances of bank runs in India, albeit to a limited extent. In September 2008, there was a rumour that ICICI Bank would fail because its investments were hit by the Wall Street troubles. Some panic set in and depositors started withdrawing cash from many ATMs in the country. Both RBI and ICICI had to come out with statements assuring the depositors that the bank had sufficient liquidity. Similarly, in 2001, financial troubles had caused a temporary run on some banks, such as, Kalupur Commercial Cooperative Bank in Gujarat.

However, the statutory requirements of CRR, SLR, and deposit insurance have instilled sufficient confidence in the minds of the public, and, therefore, bank runs are a rarity in India. Today, all the scheduled banks in India, namely, the private sector banks, such as ICICI Bank, Yes Bank, IndusInd Bank; the public sector banks, such as the State Bank of India (SBI), Punjab National Bank, Bank of Baroda, Bank of Maharashtra; and all the cooperative banks are regulated by the RBI. Public sector banks form a substantive part of the Indian banking system, as fourteen major commercial banks were nationalized by the government in 1969 and a few more in 1980. The government, under the prime ministership of Indira Gandhi, felt that banks were not serving the priority sectors of society and that India could reach commanding heights through the nationalization of banks. Of course, public sector banks have had challenges in terms of bureaucratization of administration, unionization, and non-performing assets (loans). They had to be recapitalized from time to time through

## Bank Failures and the Great Depression

In the early 1930s, the world economy in general and the US economy in particular faced one of its worst economic crises, commonly known as the Great Depression. A 'great depression' is the description of a phenomenon where GDP, employment, and prices in the economy fall quite drastically and remain at that level for a number of years. It started in 1929 and, within a few years, production and employment fell by about 25 percent. Economists offer quite a few reasons for the occurrence of the great depression. Among other, this massive fall was triggered initially by over-investment in the housing industry which was financed mainly by banks. Immigration to US too slowed down considerably after the First World War causing a fall in demand for housing.

When the construction industry faced a relative slack in the demand for housing, realty prices started going down and both the realtors and the consumers could not repay bank loans. With loan defaults becoming common, banks were reluctant to give new loans and bank customers too felt that their money was not safe in the banks. Customers began queuing outside banks to withdraw cash, but the banks were unable to honour cash withdrawal requests. As panic spread, there was a run on the banks—people started to withdraw cash, making the financial situation of banks quite precarious. The banks started holding large stocks of cash, which resulted in the lowering of loans and chequable deposits causing the money supply to fall. As the supply fell relative to the demand for money, people started selling bonds in the market to satisfy their need for money. The rapid sale of bonds resulted in a fall in the prices of bonds. As bond prices fell, interest rates started going up, which further reduced private investment, employment and output, fuelling the economic depression.

budgetary support by the union government. Moreover, there was resistance to computerization in public sector banks which delayed the much-desired efficiency gains. Today, however, things are very different. The government has allowed up to 49 percent ownership of the public sector banks in private hands. Also, the competition by the private sector banks has driven the public sector banks to become efficient.

## THE STOCK MARKET

When defining money at the beginning of this chapter, we made a distinction between income, wealth, and money. Money is essentially a medium of exchange and it also functions as a temporary store of value. Liquid funds, such as, cash on hand with the public and the chequable bank deposits certainly fall in this category. However, the savings of a household would be larger than what is held in the form of cash or chequable deposits. Essentially, out of the total income of a household during a year, a part is spent on taxes. The income which remains after deducting taxes is called disposable income, that is, income that is available for spending on goods and services. What remains out of the disposable income, after a household spends on goods and services, is the savings of the household. These savings, besides holding in the form of money, can be invested in various real and financial assets. While the real assets include assets such as property and precious metals, financial assets are various instruments including but not limited to provident fund, public provident fund (PPF), government securities, fixed deposits with firms, debentures and shares of firms, mutual funds, derivatives of shares such as SENSEX and NIFTY, and precious metal derivatives such as gold bonds. Since we are discussing stock market, let us understand more about the financial instruments below.

Many of the financial instruments are bought and sold on stock exchanges. Among the financial instruments mentioned above, the government securities are, as the name suggests, a form of loan by the public to the government. They are considered almost-risk-free assets, for the government is not expected to default on the periodic payment of interest or the repayment of borrowed funds on maturity. Debentures are also a form of loan by the public, but, given to private firms. The risk associated with debentures is somewhat higher but the interest earned on debentures is also higher than on government securities. Of course, debenture holders receive interest irrespective of whether or not a firm makes higher or lower profits, or makes profits at all. People also invest in gold and other precious metals. However, they need not buy and sell physical quantities of these metals anymore. Gold bonds, which indicate the value of gold that a purchaser holds, can be bought and sold in the market, thereby avoiding the physical handling of the precious metal.

The essence of the stock market, however, is trading in the shares of firms which collectively constitute the ownership capital of the firms, called stock, and hence the term, stock market. There is an important difference between the financial instruments mentioned above and the shares of a firm. The owners of the shares of a firm are also the owners of the firm. Those who give loans to firms in various ways, including buying debentures or keeping fixed deposits, are the creditors or lenders to the firm; they are not the owners of the firm. Therefore, irrespective of whether or not the firm makes profit, they have a first claim for receiving interest on or repayment of their financial investment. Extending that logic, the owners of the firm, that is, the shareholders are the residual claimants of the profits made by the firms. This residual amount received by the shareholders is called dividend. If a firm makes huge profits, shareholders earn large dividends, much larger than the interest that lenders earn by giving credit to the firm. On the other hand, if a firm makes losses, shareholders earn no dividend, while lenders must be paid their interest. What one learns from this is that shares are a very risky asset, for dividends depend on the fortunes of a firm.

You may be interested in knowing how stock markets evolved in the first place. To understand this, we have to go back in time—at least four centuries—to the East India Company. Of course, most of us know our history well—the

British arrived in India circa 1600 CE as traders and eventually turned masters. But the important piece of information for us is that they came as traders. Those who were interested in trading with India formed a company called the British East India Company. Others, who wanted to make a fortune in this venture, could join the company as owners if they contributed to the financial stock of the company. The risks were high but so were the returns. Eventually, many companies were formed in this manner, either for trade or for producing goods. These companies or firms had to be registered with the government so that they could officially raise financial stock or capital for their firm. Similarly, those who owned the stocks of a firm but wanted to get out of it, or those who wanted to invest and become owners of an existing firm, required a marketplace where they could buy and sell the shares of the financial stock. This need for raising initial stock or capital for firms and the need to trade in the shares of existing stock led to the formation of stock exchanges.

Many of today's institutional arrangements are inherited by India from the British—political, administrative, educational, military, and financial. It should not come as a surprise, therefore, that the Bombay Stock Exchange (BSE) is the oldest stock market in Asia and was established in Mumbai during the British rule. Its origin can be traced to the 1850s, when share brokers used to gather under a banyan tree for trading, and they formed an official organization in 1875 known as The Native Share and Stock Brokers' Association. After Independence, BSE was the first in the country to be granted permanent recognition under the Securities Contracts (Regulation) Act of 1956. While many smaller stock exchanges emerged later in different cities, BSE was the dominant player until the 1990s, which saw the emergence of another stock exchange—the National Stock Exchange (NSE) which is also based in Mumbai. A healthy competition between these two stock exchanges and the financial liberalization initiated by the government has resulted in many innovative changes in the Indian stock market in the last decade. For example, since 2005, BSE has been working professionally as a corporate entity and not just an association of stockbrokers. Today, India's stock markets have a computerized trading system, and one does not have to hold physical paper as a proof of holding stocks. All entries of ownership are recorded through computerized accounts. Moreover, the formation of and trading in mutual funds has made it easier for small investors to park their savings in the stock market.

What are mutual funds? Traditionally, people used to trade in individual shares of firms. However, this entailed people gathering information about different firms, a very difficult and time-consuming exercise. People working hard throughout the day in their respective occupations cannot afford to spend hours collecting information regarding the financial prospects of various firms and the expected price of their shares. Therefore, specialized firms evolved into what are called mutual fund managers, which invest in shares on behalf of small individual customers. Individuals invest in the mutual funds of these specialized financial firms which, in turn, invest in shares of different companies on behalf of the individual customers. Mutual funds have come as a big relief to small investors who can take advantage of the expertise of mutual fund managers in getting a sound return on their financial investments.

SENSEX and NIFTY are indices based on the value of shares of prominent firms. SENSEX is a share price index of thirty sensitive and actively traded shares on the Bombay

---

### Bulls and Bears in Dalal Street and Share Prices

For more than a century, up to the 1990s, the Bombay Stock Exchange (BSE) represented the Indian stock market. In 1928, a plot of land in Mumbai—where it still stands today—was acquired for it, and the adjoining street was named Dalal Street. 'Dalal' in several Indian languages means a trader or a broker, and hence the name. Today, the term Dalal Street has come to represent the vibrant Indian stock market, which includes both BSE and the NSE which is also situated in Mumbai.

Public limited joint stock companies are registered and listed with stock exchanges and they can raise their ownership capital through what is called Initial Public Offer (IPO), where the public can contribute to the stock of a company by subscribing to and purchasing newly issued shares. Similarly, the public can also trade in the existing shares of listed companies. The trading is done through the dalals or the share/stock brokers. Informally, share brokers and their clients are classified as either bulls or bears

---

depending upon their sentiment about share prices. Those who expect share prices to go up and hence are likely to buy shares are termed 'bulls'. Those who expect prices to fall and hence either wait to buy shares and/or sell shares are termed 'bears'. If the share prices keep going up, the market is collectively termed a 'bullish market'; if the share prices keep going down, it is termed a 'bearish market'. The terms bull and bear are used metaphorically. A charging bull raises its head and thrusts its horns up in the air signifying rising share prices; on the other hand, a bear mauls or swipes its opponent down, indicating falling share prices.

You may find it interesting to know why share prices rise or fall. Individuals invest in stocks to earn return on financial investment in the form of dividend. If a firm or the economy is doing well and expected to perform better in future, then a potential investor expects much better dividends today and in future. Therefore, the demand for shares goes up. As the demand for shares goes up, so do the share prices. If the bulls in the market expect prices to go up further, they will buy now and sell later for a profit. This adds to the demand for shares and the share prices continue to rise. Therefore, rising stock prices are an indicator of public perception and sentiment that the firms or the economy will perform better in future. Conversely, when investors perceive that a firm or the economy is not doing well and expected to perform poorly in future, they expect lower dividends, and hence sell the shares, causing their prices to fall. If the bears expect the prices to fall further, they sell the shares hoping to avoid losses. This causes prices to fall further. Thus, it is the collective expectations of a rise or fall in share prices that lead to a rise or fall in share prices!

Stock Exchange. NIFTY is an acronym for National Fifty, an index based on fifty shares traded on the National Stock Exchange of India which covers twenty-one different sectors of the Indian economy. Since these indices show the general trend of the stock market, they are also called derivatives, where investors can trade in these indices.

## PRACTICAL IMPLICATIONS FOR US

The old French proverb that was quoted at the beginning of this chapter perhaps alludes to the fact that one must save and invest, maybe in a bank, but that the savings must be used productively during one's lifetime. With what we have gathered in this chapter, perhaps the modern interpretation of the saying would suggest that the cash on hand and the funds we keep in the banks in chequable accounts are only a medium of exchange and a temporary abode of purchasing power, called money. That is, we park a part of our savings in the form of cash or a bank account, only to the extent that we demand money for transactions purpose, precautionary purpose, and some for making speculative investments. The rest of the savings may be held in the form of real assets and various financial instruments we discussed above.

How much and in which form of financial instrument one should invest depends upon the interest rates offered, tax exemptions given by the government, the risk associated with financial investments, one's own perception about the likely dividends, and expected prices of financial instruments on the stock market. One rule of thumb is to diversify your financial investments in various forms of instruments. Allocating funds to the provident fund created by your employer saves you income tax. So do other tax-deductible investment options such as PPF. If you think you have sufficient time to gather information about firms and their performance, you can invest in shares of firms and try to earn better dividends. If you are a risk-taker, you can spend time watching share prices; learn more about firms and the economic situation of the country; form expectations about future prices of shares and make a profit by buying stocks at low prices and selling when stock prices rise. But, *caveat emptor*! Consumer, beware! These are risky investments. Instead, you could think of investing in mutual funds. A parting word—generally, one does not have too much time to assess the market situation. Check with your chartered accountant or a reputed share broker for advice. Listen to the advice, make an informed judgement, and invest accordingly.

We have understood one important piece of information about banks. Banks may not have all the cash you have deposited into your account, for they do not keep your cash idle. Multiple-deposit creation occurs as banks start lending your bank balance to firms and other borrowers. However, the banking system does work, since all of us do not withdraw cash at the same time, and, all of us do not withdraw all the cash at one time. Moreover, we have faith in our banking system, and we do not expect a run on the banks. This faith in the banking system is strengthened by the stipulations of RBI regarding CRR, SLR, and the deposit insurance scheme.

Therefore, when choosing a bank, one can depend, *ceteris paribus*, upon the convenience, the consumer-friendly services and features, and past performance of the bank.

Lastly, we also know now that RBI can change the money supply in the economy by altering the CRR or SLR requirements for commercial banks. For example, a lowering of CRR would imply that more cash from a fresh deposit is available to banks to be further lent out to firms. More loans to firms implies more bank deposits from firms, and, therefore, a bigger money supply (remember, chequable deposits are a part of the money supply, M1). RBI has changed the CRR and SLR rates over time. This results in a change in the money supply. In fact, there are a few other important ways in which RBI changes the money supply in the economy. Why would RBI like to change the money supply? Discussion of this issue is related to RBI's monetary policy, to which we will return in later chapters.

## REFERENCES:

Bombay Stock Exchange (BSE), (2011), 'Heritage', http://www.bseindia.com/about/Heritage.asp

Reserve Bank of India (RBI), (2011), Frequently Asked Questions, http://www.rbi.org.in/commonman/English/ Scripts/FAQs.aspx

Securities and Exchange Board of India (SEBI), (2004), 'Glossary of Capital Markets', http://www.sebi.gov.in/bulletin/glossary.pdf

# READY RECKONER

**Bank run:** A panic situation where deposit holders queue up *en masse* at banks to withdraw cash from their accounts due to a fear that the banks may not have sufficient funds.

**Bearish stock market:** Description of a stock market, where the collective sentiment about the current and future performance of firms and the economy is negative, and results in falling share prices.

**Bullish stock market:** Description of a stock market, where the collective sentiment about the current and future performance of firms and the economy is positive, and results in rising share prices.

**CRR:** Cash Reserve Ratio. A minimum percentage of net demand and time liabilities that banks are mandated by RBI to maintain in the form of cash.

**Demand for money:** People's desire to hold money for transaction, precautionary, and speculative purposes.

**Double coincidence of wants:** The matching of mutual demands for two goods for a successful barter exchange.

**Money:** A unit of measuring value, a medium of exchange, and a store of value.

**Money Supply (M1):** Currency with the public plus chequable demand deposits with banks, plus other deposits with RBI.

**Money Supply (M3):** M1 plus time deposits with banks.

**Mutual Fund:** A financial instrument whereby specialist managers diversify risk by parking investors' funds into different stocks, hoping to offer reasonable returns to the investors.

**NIFTY:** Acronym for National Fifty, an index based on fifty shares traded on the National Stock Exchange of India which covers twenty-one different sectors of the Indian economy.

**SENSEX:** A share price index of thirty sensitive and actively traded shares on the Bombay Stock Exchange.

**Shares:** The stock of a firm divided into smaller denominations, such as, Rs 100, and traded on the stock market for a price that reflects the firm's current and future prospects and profitability.

**SLR:** Statutory Liquidity Ratio. A minimum percentage of net demand and time liabilities that banks are mandated by RBI to maintain in the form of government securities, cash on hand, and gold.

**Stock:** The capital invested in a firm by its owners.

**Stock market:** A market where shares, debentures, mutual funds, and other financial instruments are traded.

# CHAPTER 4

# FREER TRADE AND WORLD TRADE ORGANIZATION

*'It is not from the benevolence of the butcher, the brewer, or the baker, that we expect our dinner, but from their regard to their own self-interest.'*

—ADAM SMITH, *THE WEALTH OF NATIONS* (1776)

## THE BACKDROP

Circa 1776, the world was witness to several important events. Nearer home, emboldened by the victory in Bengal, the British East India Company instigated three Anglo-Maratha Wars which eventually turned India into a colony of the Company Sarkar (not the British government). On the other side of the world, the same British East India Company had monopolized the tea trade in the 'new world' colonies and, in cahoots with it, the British government had unilaterally levied high taxes on tea imports in the Americas. The Americans revolted by throwing all the tea shipments

into the sea. The event, famously known as the Boston Tea Party, eventually led to the Declaration of Independence by the American colonies (The United States of America) in 1776. And, halfway between India and America, the same year, two Scotsmen revolutionized the way we produced industrial goods, travelled, and understood the working of the economic system and the benefits of free trade.

One of them was the Scottish inventor and engineer, James Watt. He invented the steam engine which was used in factories, railways, and ocean liners (steamers), allowing larger production volumes and faster transport of goods and people than ever before. The other Scot, Adam Smith, had a profound impact on our understanding of the working of the economic system and free trade. Universally cited as the 'father of modern economics', Adam Smith wrote the famous treatise titled *An Inquiry into the Nature and Causes of the Wealth of Nations,* in 1776. The statement from his treatise quoted at the beginning of this chapter underlines the basic premise in economics—the self-interest of each economic agent compels them to specialize in the production of what they are good at and to exchange it with others to satisfy their needs. He believed that such self-interest-driven specialization and exchange maximizes a society's welfare.

### Freer Trade and Welfare Gain

Smith argued that a butcher, a brewer, and a baker specialize, respectively, in selling meat, alcohol, and bread for they are good at it, and the proceeds of selling these goods will help them buy other goods. If they were to produce all their requirements themselves, they would be producing inefficiently and, therefore, trading and consuming less of all goods. It is for this very reason that a tailor does not make his own shoes and a cobbler does not stitch his own clothes. But, what if one is good at producing two or more things? Should he produce all those things by himself? This issue was addressed by another economist, David Ricardo. He further refined Adam Smith's idea and came up with the concept of comparative advantage.

To understand the concept of comparative advantage, let us consider an example. Suppose you are a very good computer programmer compared with most others but you are an excellent entrepreneur as well. You may begin doing both, that is, writing computer programmes and being a sole proprietor (entrepreneur) selling the programmes. But, soon, you will realize that, between writing programmes and being an entrepreneur—if you are better at the latter—you will benefit from concentrating on your entrepreneurial activities by hiring full-time computer programmers. You may be a good computer programmer but you will find yourself assigning that job to others in order to concentrate on your comparative advantage—being an entrepreneur. And, those whom you hire will be more adept at being programmers than at being entrepreneurs. What is true of individuals in a firm may also be true of firms, of cities, of different states of a nation, and of two countries. Therefore, the welfare of economic agents will improve when they specialize in those activities in which they have a comparative advantage and engage in free trade through exchange among themselves. After all, comparative advantage is the reason why India specializes in and exports business process outsourcing (BPO) and software services to Germany, and imports heavy engineering goods from her.

However, it was difficult to ascertain the source of comparative advantage: Which countries would export which commodities, and which factors of production would benefit from trade? These issues were addressed in the early 1930s by two economists—Eli Heckscher and Bertil Ohlin of the Stockholm School of Economics. They advocated what is now known as the factor abundance theory or, more popularly, the Heckscher–Ohlin theory. They argued that a country will export that commodity which uses its abundant factor more intensively, and that the abundant factor will gain from trade. For example, if India is a labour-abundant country—which it is—it would export goods that use labour more intensively than capital. And it is plain to see that India's BPO industry and software industry produce and export services that use unskilled and skilled labour more intensively. Of course, trade in these services benefits labour, BPO employees, and computer programmers. Similarly, Germany and the US—labour-scarce and capital-abundant economies—produce and export capital-intensive goods, such as, heavy engineering machinery, including computer-aided machines. Clearly, countries seem to specialize in the production and export of those goods in which their abundant factor is used more intensively. And in both countries, the respective abundant factor would benefit from trade.

The theories of comparative advantage and factor abundance do explain most of the trading pattern among countries. However, some smart reader may quickly question: Then how does one explain that German cars—such as, the BMW and the Volkswagen—are quite popular in Japan, while Japanese cars—such as, the Toyota and the Nissan—are at the top in German consumer surveys? This pattern shows that goods in the same category are exported and imported between the two countries and, hence, comparative advantage or factor abundance is not the only reason for the trade in cars between Germany and Japan. Trade economists like Paul Krugman addressed this 'intra-industry' trade among countries by advocating complementary theories now christened as New Trade Theories (NTTs). The source of intra-industry trade, according to these theories, lies in the fact that consumers like a variety to choose from, and firms enjoy economies of scale by concentrating on producing large volumes of a particular variety of a good. For example, cars are a commodity which is not the same across the world. It is a differentiated product, with manufacturers distinguishing their cars from those of other manufacturers through variation in features and quality. Since consumers, who have varied tastes and preferences, value this variety, firms specialize in the production of similar, but differentiated, goods (read, cars) and enjoy economies of scale.

# FORMATION OF THE WORLD TRADE ORGANIZATION

From the above discussion, it becomes clear that countries gain from freer trade through specialization in production, arising out of comparative advantage and/or factor-abundance and/or differentiated products. However, despite the sound theoretical basis for freer trade, in reality, one finds that countries try to protect their own domestic markets by discouraging imports and exports. Such discouragement takes various forms: bans or quota restrictions on import volumes; making foreign exporters agree to Voluntary Export Restraints (VERs); high customs duties (tariffs) on imported products; and Non-Tariff Barriers (NTBs) in the form of stricter quality specifications on imports.

For example, in the early 1980s, threatened by a surge in the import of fuel-efficient and cheaper Japanese cars into the US, a VER agreement was signed between the US and Japan, limiting Japanese exports to 1.68 million cars annually, virtually imposing a quota limit on imports. In the early 1990s, the US banned import of beef from Britain, alleging that the cows in Britain were suffering from Mad Cow Disease. A little later, almost reciprocally, Britain and other European countries banned the import of beef from the US; it was argued that US beef contained growth hormones which are harmful to humans. Whether or not such reciprocal bans are legitimate and have a scientific basis is a debatable issue. Similarly, at various times, the export of Indian garments to the US has been restricted on the grounds that they were inflammable. Whether this is a genuine concern or a thinly veiled protection of the US domestic industry, again, becomes a debatable issue. Such NTBs are not recent phenomena, they have been exercised by many countries in the early part of the twentieth century. In addition, traditionally, most countries have levied high customs duties (import tariffs) to protect domestic markets. In the second half of the twentieth century, customs duties on quite a few products were higher than 100 percent. Obviously, the objective behind high customs duties was not revenue generation but protection of domestic markets.

During the two world wars, the industrialized countries followed a different form of protection of domestic industries. Europe and America devalued their currencies in the hope that it would promote exports. How? Let us suppose, for example, that in 1933, one British pound sterling equalled four US dollars. If, the following year, the US government were to make its central bank buy a large amount of British pounds at the rate of five US dollars to one British pound, it could force all the others to buy and sell at the rate of one British pound for five US dollars. Thereby, the US dollar would get devalued by 25 percent. Once the US dollar was devalued against the British pound, US producers would be able to export more since one British pound could then buy more goods from the US. The increase in exports would give a boost to domestic production and employment in the US but would, perhaps, lead to reduced production and a lower rate of employment in Great Britain. If only the US were to devalue its currency, the perceived benefits may accrue to her. However, if all countries, in a competitive behaviour, devalue their currencies in the hope of improving the lot of their own citizens, no country benefits in the end. In fact, competitive devaluation creates uncertainty in the foreign exchange market and lessens incentives for trade among nations.

Competitive efforts by various countries, consisting of imposition of quotas, VERs, bans, and high customs duties, in general, and the devaluation of their respective currencies, in particular, are termed as beggar-thy-neighbour policies. They are so called because each country tries to offer an advantage to the domestic industry at the cost of other countries. In the process—when every country does this—it leads to an almost autarkic (no-trade among countries) situation, and worsens trade, production, and employment prospects everywhere. Beggar-thy-neighbour policies such as these prevailed after World War I, and the resultant loss of markets was one of the reasons—if not the only one—that led countries to World War II. The reality check and implications were not lost on the world leaders. Towards the end of the war, they gathered in Bretton Woods, New Hampshire, USA, in July 1944. The gathering—popularly known as the Bretton Woods Conference—was held out of an expressed need to establish international organizations that would facilitate and regulate international trade and the monetary and financial environment.

Two international organizations were born out of the deliberations of the Bretton Woods Conference—one was the International Bank for Reconstruction and Development (IBRD), namely, the World Bank, and the other was the International Monetary Fund (IMF). The World Bank was to help the war-ravaged Western world in its reconstruction and the third world countries in their development programmes while IMF was to take care of the issues of balance of payment and exchange rate management among the countries. The idea of a third organization—the International Trade Organization (ITO)—was also conceived during the Conference, but it had an abortive beginning due to continued resistance by the US Congress. Instead, what transpired, by 1948, was the General Agreement on Tariff and Trade (GATT). ITO would have been an organization, complementing the other two Bretton Woods-proposed international bodies—IMF and the World Bank. What came about, instead, was a mere agreement on tariffs and trade. GATT did not have the teeth to promote trade liberalization which an organization like ITO would have had.

GATT did, however, take the trade liberalization efforts forward. Under the auspices of this agreement, industrial tariffs among the developed countries came down substantially. By 1979, seven rounds of trade negotiations had been carried out, leading to the reduction of industrial tariffs among major industrial markets to a mere 4.7 percent. The number of member countries increased from the original 23 in 1948 to over 102 by the end of the seventh round in 1979. However, as mentioned earlier, GATT did not have the status of an organization and, therefore, it became very difficult to take every country along the path of liberalization, to implement what was agreed upon, and to settle disputes among the countries. Moreover, many traditional markets—such as agriculture and textiles—were outside the purview of GATT; and many new markets—such as intellectual property and services—were addressed inadequately. Therefore, member countries now felt the need to have a global organization which would cover trade liberalization over a comprehensive range of goods and services, and would also address issues of dispute settlement. Towards this end, the eighth round of trade negotiations under the auspices of GATT began in Punta del Este in the Latin American country, Uruguay. The negotiations continued from September 1986 to April

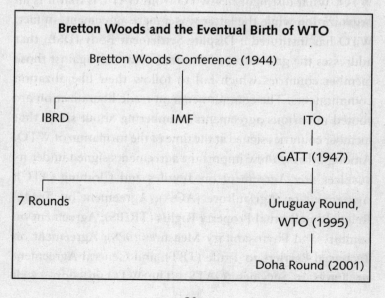

**Bretton Woods and the Eventual Birth of WTO**

Bretton Woods Conference (1944)

IBRD      IMF      ITO

GATT (1947)

7 Rounds      Uruguay Round, WTO (1995)

Doha Round (2001)

1994 and, at the conclusion of the Uruguay Round, member countries agreed to establish an organization, the WTO, which came into being from January 1, 1995, with its headquarters in Geneva, Switzerland.

## The Working of WTO

As of 2008, more than 153 countries had become members of WTO. China was reluctant to join it in 1995; however, having considered the mutual benefits that accrue to member countries, she became a member in 2001. And, as we read, by the close of 2012, the Russian Federation will have been inducted into WTO. Only a few countries, such as, Iran and Iraq, still remain outside the purview of WTO. What distinguishes WTO from GATT is that it is an organization while the latter was a mere agreement. In fact, WTO has instituted a Dispute Settlement Body (DSB) that addresses the grievances of member countries against those member countries which fail to follow their liberalization commitments. The commitments on trade liberalization are rooted in various agreements (numbering about sixty) that member countries signed at the time of the formation of WTO. Among others, a few important agreements signed under its auspices are: Agreement on Textiles and Clothing (ATC); Agreement on Agriculture (AOA); Agreement on Trade-Related Intellectual Property Rights (TRIPS); Agreement on Sanitary and Phytosanitary Measures (SPS); Agreement on Technical Barriers to Trade (TBT); and General Agreement on Trade in Services (GATS). The WTO mission—well grounded in trade theories—is to facilitate the smooth flow of trade among countries. To this end, the general purpose of all the agreements is to remove quantitative restrictions such as import bans or quota; to ease customs duty protection for domestic industry; to reduce subsidies on production and/or exports; and to harmonize product standards and specifications on a scientific basis so that trade is not withheld due to ad hoc non-tariff barriers.

For example, under ATC, all the quota restrictions that member countries had placed on import of textiles and clothing under the earlier Multi-Fibre Agreement (MFA) were set to terminate within ten years from the formation of WTO. As a result of this, today, the textiles and clothing sector is completely free of all quota restrictions on imports. Before the formation of WTO, Indian exports were constrained by import quotas imposed by the developed world. Today, no such constraints hamper India's apparent exports. A few years ago, the US had banned import of shrimps from India and a few other countries on the grounds that the harvesting of shrimps as carried out by them was damaging the environment. The argument was that the fisherfolk in these countries were not using turtle-excluding devices (TEDs) while, in the US, domestic laws had made the use of TEDs mandatory while harvesting shrimps. As stated earlier, bans such as this are called non-tariff barriers (NTBs) to trade, and issues related to them are addressed in the SPS and the TBT Agreements of WTO. The countries so affected took the matter to the DSB of WTO. Referring to Articles XI and

XX of GATT, DSB ruled that, since the US did not apply the restrictions to Caribbean countries, the ban was an arbitrary and unjustifiable discrimination between countries. Moreover, the deliberations also proffered the view that fisherfolk may not need to use TEDs if they were employing a different production and processing method (PPM) which would lead to a similar, or better, level of turtle protection. In the US, deep-sea fishing with mechanized trawlers does cause environmental damage because turtles, too, get caught during harvesting. Indian fisherfolk, on the other hand, engage in traditional harvesting practices in brackish water and coastal fishing, which may not require TEDs.

The TRIPS Agreement, too, has had an impact on trading norms. This agreement has helped member nations harmonize their domestic laws on intellectual property rights. Prior to WTO, patent rights in different countries were granted for different durations of time. Moreover, some countries had both process patents and product patents, while others had only process patents. With the implementation of the TRIPS Agreement, harmonization has been ushered in. Among other things, for example, patent rights are now granted for twenty years in all member countries, for whom, having process and product patents both in place is obligatory. Such organization of patent laws offers an incentive for innovation as well as a smooth trade of patented goods across nations. The TRIPS Agreement also facilitates countries in maintaining a registry of goods with unique Geographic Indicators (GIs). With this registry, countries can prevent other countries from producing and exporting GI-registered goods. For example, Darjeeling tea, Hapus (Alphonso) mangoes, Basmati rice, and quite a few other products that form the national registry in India can be produced in and exported from India only (except Basmati rice which can be exported from Pakistan too). This means that no other country can claim to produce these goods as its own and under that specific name. At the heart of the GI registry is the fact that the distinctive characteristics and the appellation of some products are derived from the geography, climate, soil, and method of production unique to a particular location. The distinctiveness of such products and of the location of their production must, therefore, be protected against spurious products from elsewhere masquerading as the original products.

Another—and one of the most important agreements signed under the auspices of WTO—is the Agreement on Agriculture (AOA). To provide market access and export competition, AOA stipulated that developed countries would lower their customs duties on imports as well as the export subsidies by 36 percent over a six-year period starting 1995. Similarly, developing countries would lower their customs duties on imports as well as the export subsidies by 24 percent over a ten-year period starting 1995. An important distortion in the global trade in agriculture also arises due to domestic subsidy supports. These supports are either product-specific—such as minimum support prices for agricultural commodities—or non-product-specific—such as subsidy provision for electricity, fertilizers, and other inputs. For developed countries, product-specific and non-product-specific support to agriculture—each of which was in excess of 5 percent of the value of the total agricultural produce—was defined as the Aggregate Measure of Support (AMS). The AMS thus arrived at was to be reduced by 20 percent over a period of six years for developed countries. For developing countries, AMS was defined as the product-specific and non-product-specific support to agriculture—each of which was in excess of 10 percent of the value of the total agricultural produce. The AMS for developing countries was to be reduced by 13.3 percent over a period of ten years. Here, India did not have any reduction commitments, since the AMS for India was below 10 percent of the value of the agricultural produce.

## Implementation Issues and the Future

In quite a few areas, WTO agreements have made a significant progress in trade liberalization. As shown earlier, the establishment of DSB has helped member countries, including many developing countries, to prevent a recurrence of NTBs to their exports. Similarly, the highly restrictive trading arrangements that prevailed prior to the establishment of WTO have been eliminated and, now, there are no country-specific import quota restrictions on the export of textiles and clothing from developing countries. Again, as stated earlier, the tariffs on industrial products have been brought down significantly by developed countries. For example, by the year 2009, the US had brought down its average applied customs duties on the import of manufactured goods to 2.6

## India and Pakistan: Enemies Turn Most Favoured Nations (MFNs)!

In early November 2011, Indians and Pakistanis were shocked to read in the newspapers that Pakistan had also finally decided to grant the MFN status to India, the process of which will be completed by end of 2012. Why also and finally? Because, people on both sides of the border had been equally shocked some sixteen years earlier, when India had unilaterally granted MFN status to Pakistan in 1996, immediately after the formation of WTO.

How is it possible that India grants MFN status to its arch enemy Pakistan and Pakistan too hopes to reciprocate the gesture albeit belatedly? The mystery is solved once we understand the meaning of the term MFN. About sixty agreements have been signed under the auspices of WTO, some of which have been referred to elsewhere in this chapter. All these agreements are characterized by a few important WTO principles that were originally enshrined in GATT articles. For example, a hallmark of WTO is the principle of non-discrimination among member countries. This principle, christened as the MFN principle in Article I of GATT, mandates that the trade policy treatment which a member country metes out to its most favoured nation should also be meted out to all other member countries. In essence, simply put, it means that all member countries have to be given MFN status. For example, if India removes quota restrictions on the import of agricultural products from a particular country, the quota removal must apply to all the other member countries as well.

You may now wonder—since the MFN clause implies treating all countries equally in terms of trade policies—why it is necessary to make the special effort of granting MFN status to specific countries, say, to a country like Pakistan. The catch is that an exemption is granted by Article XXI of GATT which allows member countries to apply trade controls if they are deemed necessary due to concerns of national security. By not granting each other MFN status in 1995, both India and Pakistan had exercised the use of this exemption at the time of the formation of WTO.

By granting MFN status to Pakistan a year after the formation of WTO, India agreed to extend the same treatment to Pakistan as it would to other countries. This did not imply any special treatment or 'most favoured treatment' as the name mistakenly suggests. Perhaps Indian politicians used this MFN terminology to their own advantage for improving diplomatic relations with Pakistan. Pakistan seems to be doing the same albeit belatedly. One thing is for sure, though—businessmen and consumers on both sides were happy. Indians would get—among other things—competitively priced cotton yarn, textiles, leather goods and furniture in general; and during times of shortage, onions in particular! Similarly, Pakistanis would get—again, among other things—competitively priced vegetables, engineering goods and tea in general; and during times of shortage, sugar in particular.

percent, and that on agricultural products to 4.7 percent. The TRIPS Agreement has also helped coordinate intellectual property rights across countries. To the extent of what has been described above, WTO has made a significant impact on trade liberalization. However, there were many issues on which developed and developing countries disagreed on the modalities of implementation of WTO norms. Therefore, to address these issues and to carry the reforms further, WTO began its ninth round of trade negotiations in 2001. This latest round of trade negotiations began in Doha and, therefore, this round was christened as the Doha Round.

The Doha Round has not been concluded so far. Given that the preceding Uruguay Round was concluded within eight years, the Doha Round certainly seems to have got delayed. There are several reasons for it. While, at a systemic level, all countries agree that trade liberalization is good, at the individual (read, country) level, there is always a motivation to give less to, and get more from, other countries. This tendency gets accentuated when countries suffer from severe recession as they have, during the last few years. For example, since the year 2007, the US and European countries have experienced high unemployment rates. In times of exigency, the domestic industrial and farming communities tend to lobby hard to protect domestic stakeholders, pushing WTO-led reforms to the backburner. Moreover, in the Uruguay Round, developing countries did not have the requisite experience in negotiations and prior preparations for drafting mutually beneficial economic agreements. On the other hand, Western countries had significant experience on account of the processes that had led to the formation of economic groupings, such as, the North American Free Trade Agreement (NAFTA) and the European Union (EU). Now that developing countries, too, are sufficiently experienced, the negotiations are getting protracted this time around. Hopefully, the negotiators of all the countries will soon reach a consensus. It remains to be seen what the important issues are, in the current Doha Round, and in what way they may affect us.

## CUSTOMS DUTIES

Developed countries believe that they have quite significantly reduced their customs duties on imported products. However, developing countries do not seem to allow enough market access to the developed ones. For example, while it is true that the prevailing applied customs duties in India are lower than what they used to be in the past, they are, nevertheless, higher than in the Western world. By the year 2009, India's average applied customs duties on imports had come down to 32 percent for the agricultural sector and 10 percent for the non-agricultural sector. However, they are still relatively quite high compared to those in the US which are as low as about 5 percent. Moreover, while the actual customs duties might be somewhat lower in India, the 'bound rates' of customs duties—the maximum rates of customs duties which a country may charge on imported goods—are very high. The bound rates are naturally higher than the actual customs duties charged by a country. The average bound rates for agricultural imports are still above 113 percent in India. In fact, the maximum bound rate for animal products, dairy products, and fruits and vegetables is 150 percent. Therefore, in the Doha Round, one of the expectations of the developed countries is that the developing countries give better market access to them.

## SUBSIDIES

While the developed countries point at the high customs duties, the developing countries are quick to point at the humongous subsidies that the former grant to their agriculture sector, and the procedural loopholes that they use to avoid reducing their subsidies. To arrive at AMS to domestic agriculture in the base year, certain exemptions were given to all countries. These included the Green Box subsidies which cover expenditures on, for example, agricultural research, extension activities, and environmental protection measures. Moreover, while calculating the current yearly AMS, some other forms of subsidies were not to be included in the current AMS calculations. These included Blue Box Subsidies which cover payments made by the state to farmers for limiting their production. This, of course, would show lower levels of AMS compared to the base-period AMS.

Furthermore, as it happened, agricultural prices in the year which was chosen for the calculation of the base-year AMS were quite low. And, a country would naturally give high levels of support to farmers when agricultural prices are very low. So, the base-year AMS was too high to start with. Over time, as agricultural prices improved, there was less need to give subsidies. Overall, therefore, it appeared on paper that the Western countries had reduced their subsidies considerably. For example, AMS for the US in the base year (1986–88, when prices were very low) was $22.2 billion. This AMS had to be reduced by 20 percent over six years after the formation of WTO. However, within a few years, AMS came down to $14 billion, much lower than the expected 20 percent reduction. It was no surprise that the choice of the base year and the exclusion of Blue Box subsidies from the calculation of the current AMS had done the trick. In contrast, developing countries had practically no commitments to reduce subsidies since their expenditure on subsidies was low. Having learnt this the hard way, developing countries will not accept many other demands during the Doha Round, unless the developed countries place serious commitments on the table to reduce subsidies.

The developed countries are also very aggressive about opening up the services sector. While the GATS and the one on investments have not made a significant or affirmative advance in the Doha Round, India, on its own, has, over time, cautiously opened up some of the service sectors. Currently, the insurance sector allows 26 percent FDI, and the banking sector, 49 percent. FDI in media, such as, newsprint and radio news broadcasting, has been kept completely at bay. If the foreign universities bill—which is being tabled in Parliament—is any indication, domestic educational institutions are likely to face healthy competition from foreign universities. While such progressive liberalization has not been formally concluded in the current Doha Round, developing countries are not likely to yield unless they can negotiate for a reciprocal opening up of the labour markets and subsidy reduction by the Western world. For example, India will expect that other countries will make it easier to get work permits for Indian nurses, teachers, software professionals and others service providers. Moreover, social security taxes may not be levied on professionals temporarily working abroad, for such professionals return to India on completion of work permits and do not depend upon the host governments to provide retirement benefits and social security. Further, to remain competitive in the educational sector, that is, offer delivery of quality education and educational infrastructure, domestic educational institutions—especially the public institutions—may have to be allowed to charge competitive fees, offer variable pay to attract the best faculty, and introduce a hire-and-fire policy to sustain academic excellence.

To sum up, the long-term objective of WTO is to ensure that international trade is conducted smoothly and predictably through negotiations among the member countries. The fear against the trading company—the British East India Company—that was generated both in America and India circa 1776 is over. Instead, the ideas propounded in that same year by Adam Smith have been successfully implemented by WTO. No doubt, the transition is a slow process, since it is not easy for governments to satisfy all the stakeholders at once. As the current Doha Round has been progressing very slowly, groups of countries have begun

## Trade War over Chicken Feet aka Phoenix Talons!

Since August 2010, hatcheries from Mangalore have been exporting twenty-five tonnes of chicken feet (claws) every month to China. The chicken feet are a waste product for Indians but a culinary delicacy in China, and are popularly known as Phoenix Talons. To paraphrase Adam Smith, the Chinese get their Phoenix Talons, not out of the benevolence, but the self-interest, of Indian hatcheries. Since chicken feet are one of the joint products—the others being breasts, legs (drum sticks), and feathers—the cost of preparing market-ready Phoenix Talons is extremely low, and the Chinese find both the price and the product very attractive. International trade makes good business sense, indeed!

However, about a decade ago, in an effort to restrict cheap imports of poultry products from the US, India increased its customs duties on the import of poultry products from 35 percent to 100 percent. This was possible thanks to the very high level of bound customs duties submitted by India in its tariff schedule to WTO. The domestic poultry industry hailed the decision by arguing that the US was trying to dump poultry products, such as, chicken legs, in India. It was contended that US consumers preferred breast meat to other parts of poultry, and therefore, the cheap non-breast portions were being dumped in the rest of the world. One wonders as to what was wrong in allowing poor Indians to get their protein delicacy—chicken legs—at a cheaper rate. Perhaps the half-a-billion consumers were not organized and hence could not prevent the rise in duty. Or perhaps, a handful of influential poultry operators were able to influence government policy. If the concern was for Indians as a whole, then perhaps, some inefficient hatcheries in India would have exited the market; their resources could have been put to some better use elsewhere; and Indian consumers would pay a much lower price for their delicacy. In the same vein, would the domestic poultry operators accuse enterprising Mangalore hatcheries of dumping chicken feet in China?

In this context, it is useful to know that WTO allows imposition of Anti-Dumping duties. Dumping has a special meaning in WTO agreements. If an exporter sells a good in a foreign market for a CIF (cost, insurance, freight) price which is lower than its normal value in the exporter's domestic market, it is considered as 'dumping'. Essentially, the normal value refers to the fact that the domestic price (in exporter's market) is not lower than the cost of production. Do you think that the Mangalore hatcheries and the US exporters were dumping poultry products in China and India, respectively? That products were being sold at a price below the cost of production? Incidentally, in 2010, China imposed an anti-dumping duty on US exports of poultry products (read Phoenix Talons) to China, and the US has already challenged the move in accordance with the WTO process under DSB. It appears that US too is likely to take India to WTO on the issue of market access for chicken products. Further, if China also imposes anti-dumping duty on India's exports of Phoenix Talons, we are likely to witness a full-scale trade war.

to form Free Trade Areas (FTAs). While WTO does not encourage this, it allows FTAs as long as its members do not increase trade restrictions against the non-FTA countries. Liberalizing trade within FTA would be seen as a step in the right direction, leading to a broader multilateral liberalization that would come through the Doha Round. It is to be hoped that, as countries recover from the severe recession that hit them in the recent past, the world will see further substantial reductions in subsides in the developed world, a lowering of customs duties in the developing world, and mutual opening up of the service sector. In fact, very recently, India removed altogether the customs duty on the import of pulses. This was necessitated by the fact that food inflation was in double digits in India. As we conclude the discussion on WTO issues, we know that we have made oblique references to the economic phenomena of recession and inflation. It is time for us to understand these concepts as well as the policies followed by the government to eradicate them. We will take up these aspects in the following chapters.

REFERENCES:

Bernasconi-Osterwalder, N., D. Magraw, M.J. Oliva, E. Tuerk, (2006), *Environment and Trade: A Guide to WTO Jurisprudence*, UK: Earthscan

Deodhar, S., (2001), 'WTO Agreements and Indian Agriculture: Retrospection and Prospects', in *Implications of WTO Agreements for Indian Agriculture*, (eds) S. Datta and S. Deodhar, Ahmedabad: Indian Institute of Management

Krugman, P., M. Obstfeld, M. Melitz, (2011), *International Economics: Theory and Policy*, 9th Edition, Boston: Addison-Wesley

WTO, (2011), 'Understanding the WTO', http://www.wto.org/english/thewto_e/whatis _e/tif_e/tif_e.htm

———, (2010), *World Tariff Profiles*, Geneva: World Trade Organization and International Trade Centre

# READY RECKONER

**Anti-dumpting duty:** Duty charged by a government on a product that is imported from a foreign firm and that is being sold at a price below the normal value in the exporter's domestic market. The duty would be equal to the difference between the exporter's price in the importing country and the normal value of the product in the exporter's domestic market.

**Beggar-thy-neighbour policy:** Policy followed by many countries to competitively devalue their currencies in order to gain advantage in exports. Competitive restrictions on trade, such as, import bans, quotas, and the imposition of high customs duties, are also sometimes described by this term.

**Comparative advantage:** A factual description where a person, a firm, or a country has the ability to produce two (or more) goods, though it is relatively more efficient in producing one of them.

**Customs duty:** Duty charged by a country on a product before its entry into the domestic market. Sometimes, the term is also referred to as import tariff or just tariff.

**Dumping:** Selling a product in an importing country for a price which is lower than the normal value in the exporter's domestic market. Normal value generally refers to a price in the ordinary business of trade in the exporter's domestic market (which is not lower than the cost of production).

**Factor Abundance Theory:** See Heckscher–Ohlin Theory.

**Free Trade Area (FTA):** As per GATT Article XXIV-8(b), an FTA is a group of two or more countries in which customs duties and other restrictive regulations of commerce are eliminated on substantial trade between these countries for the products originating in these countries.

**Heckscher–Ohlin Theory:** A trade theory which postulates that a country will export that commodity which uses its abundant factor more intensively.

**Import tariff or import duty:** see Customs duty.

**Intra-industry trade:** Trade among nations in similar but differentiated products.

**Most Favoured Nation (MFN):** MFN refers to the principle that forms Article I of GATT. This principle mandates that, whatever trade policy treatment a member country metes out to its most favoured nation, the same treatment should be meted out to all other member countries. In essence, simply put, it means that all member countries have to be given MFN status. Alternately, this is also referred to as the non-discrimination principle.

**New Trade Theories (NTTs):** Trade theories that rely on a preference for variety on the part of consumers and the existence of economies of scale that lead to intra-industry trade.

**Non-Tariff Barriers (NTBs):** NTBs are the barriers to import in a country—other than customs duties—and which, among others, include quotas, sanitary and phytosanitary regulations, and import licensing.

**Quota:** In the context of international trade, this refers to an upper limit set by the government of a country on the quantity of imports per year.

**Tariff:** See Customs duty.

**Voluntary Export Restraints (VERs):** Restraint sought through bilateral negotiations to persuade exporting countries to limit their exports 'voluntarily' or to agree to some other means of sharing markets, with a view to protecting domestic industry. WTO does not allow continuance of VERs. Instead, some form of special safeguard is allowed for a maximum period of four years if VERs exist, predating the formation of WTO.

# CHAPTER 5

# ANATOMY OF INFLATION

*'Inflation is the one form of taxation that can be imposed without legislation.'*

—MILTON FRIEDMAN

## WHAT IS INFLATION?

In the years 2010 and 2011, consumers were distressed by the frequent rise in the prices of goods of daily requirement. Complaints about this were commonly heard from Indian homemakers who were quick to point out that the price of dal (pulses)—a staple food and vital source of protein for a majority of Indians—had increased substantially and almost touched the high mark of Rs 100 per kg. In response, the government reduced the customs duty on imports of dal to zero, in the hope that dal prices would come down. From the previous chapter, we know that the average bound customs duty and the average actual customs duty on imports of agricultural products in India, at about 100 percent and 30 percent, respectively, are still high. This is partly to protect the domestic producers and partly to generate revenue for the government. In this context, bringing the customs duty on dal to zero was evidently an emergency step taken by a government which was seriously worried about food inflation and its electoral consequences. But, was the rise of dal price an isolated case? How critical was the problem for most commodities in general? If we go by the statistics provided by newspapers and the announcements made by the government, inflation was no longer in single digits, it hovered around 10 to 12 percent. What do these numbers tell us? They tell us that there was a sustained and overall rise in the general price level. Inflation is just that—a sustained and overall rise in the general price level.

How does one calculate the general price level and the changes in it? Let us consider a simple example. Let us suppose that a consumer's basket of commodities has only two goods—food and clothing, and that their respective prices on January 1, 2009 were Rs 80 and Rs 90, respectively. If the prices of these commodities were to rise to Rs 100 and Rs 99, respectively, by January 1, 2010, a quick calculation would tell you that the food price rose by Rs 20 representing a 25 percent rise in the price per year ([20/80] x 100). Similarly, the price rise calculation for clothing shows that the price increased by 10 percent per year ([9/90] x 100). To summarize the price rise on these two goods, the simple arithmetic average of the individual price rise—25 percent and 10 percent—can be taken, amounting to a general price rise of 17.5 percent ([25+10]/2).

However, let us consider that (25+10)/2 can also be written as (0.5) (25) + (0.5) (10), implying that equal weights of 0.5 (that is, 1/2) are assigned to both price rises, resulting in a general price rise of 17.5 percent. But this would be logical only if one spent an equal amount of income, that is, incurred an equal expenditure on the two goods. Assuming that one consumes five units of food and two units of clothing at the initial prices of Rs 80 and Rs 90, respectively, this would mean that, out of the total expenditure of Rs 580 (that is, [80x5] + [90x2]), one is spending Rs 400 on food and Rs 180 on clothing. This would imply that, in the base year, about 69 percent of the expenditure is spent on food and about 31 percent on clothing. Therefore, one would be more concerned about the price rise on food than on clothing. To capture this relative importance of food over clothing, weights of 0.69 and 0.31 can be used for the individual price rise. Hence, we improve the accuracy of the general price rise by using the weighted average of the two price rises: (0.69) (25) + (0.31) (10) = 17.25 + 3.1 = 20.35 percent. Clearly, after taking into account the relative importance of the two goods in the consumption basket, the representative general price rise or the inflation rate is higher, that is, it is not 17.5 percent but 20.35 percent.

This is how the inflation rate is calculated by the government: the weighted average of the increase in prices of different commodity groups in the consumption basket. After the inflation rate is calculated thus, the government comes up with the general price level in the economy which is referred to as the Index Number. In the calculation of an index number, its value in the reference year—or the base year—is always assumed to be 100. To find out the price level 'T' years after the base year, one simply has to add the inflation rate over those T years to the base year price level of 100. In the example given above, if we take 2009 as the base year with a general price level of 100 on January 1, then the general price level on January 1, 2010 will be 100 + 20.35 = 120.35. Ignoring the number to the right of the decimal value for a moment, if the index numbers for two successive years—2010 and 2011—were 120 and 132, respectively, it would mean that the inflation was 20 percent in 2009, and that the general price level rose by 32 percent between 2009 and 2011. Further, the inflation rate between 2010 and 2011 would be ([132-120]/120) x 100 = (12/120) x 100, which is 10 percent per year. An easy formula used to construct such index numbers was given by the German economist Étienne Laspeyres. This formula and its derivation are given in the box below.

## WHY DOES INFLATION OCCUR?

Now that we have a basic idea about how inflation is calculated, we shall shed light on why inflation occurs at all. Let us assume that prices are stable to begin with; inflation occurs when this stability is broken by a demand for goods and services in excess of the available supply over a sustained period. On the other hand, the prices of some goods may fall if their supply exceeds the market demand. However, as we know from the earlier discussion, the general price rise is the weighted average of the rise (or the fall) in prices of all the

## Laspeyres Price Index:
## An Easy Formula to Calculate Price Level

The calculation of the general price level discussed earlier in the text can be summarized in an easy formula developed by the German economist, Étienne Laspeyres. If the base year for an index number is taken as 0, and the year for which the index number is to be calculated is denoted as T, then the Laspeyres Price Index ($PI_T$) number can be easily remembered as follows:

$$PI_T = \frac{\Sigma P_T Q_0}{\Sigma P_0 Q_0} \times 100,$$

where $PI_T$ represents the price index number in the year T; $\Sigma$ represents summing over two goods—food and clothing; $P_T$ and $P_0$ represent the prices of goods in the year T and the year 0; and $Q_0$ represents the quantities of goods consumed in the year 0. The base year price index number $PI_0$ is assumed to be 100. Now, let the prices in the year T and the year 0 for food and clothing be: $P_T$ = Rs 100 and Rs 99, $P_0$ = Rs 80 and Rs 90. Further, let the base year quantities for food and clothing be: $Q_0$ = 5 and 2, respectively. One can easily verify that the price index number for the year T will be 120.34. This is arrived at in the following manner:

$$PI_T = \frac{(100 \times 5) + (99 \times 2)}{(80 \times 5) + (90 \times 2)} \times 100 = \frac{(698)}{(580)} \times 100 = 120.34$$

This indicates that the general price level in the year T is 120.34 and the inflation rate is 20.34 percent during the period 0 to T.

For those who are mathematically inclined, an involved proof of the above formula is presented below. The formula for the price index number is derived as follows: Apart from 0 and T defined above, let i be a commodity group (i = 1 to n) in the consumption basket and $w_i$ be the share of that group in the total expenditure, that is, the weight attached to the commodity group i. Then,

$$\text{Price Index, } PI_T = 100 + \sum_{i=1}^{n}\left(\frac{P_{Ti} - P_{0i}}{P_{0i}}\right) w_i \times 100,$$

where $w_i = \dfrac{P_{0i}Q_{0i}}{\Sigma_{i=1}^{n}P_{0i}Q_{0i}}$

You can verify that by substituting for $w_i$ in the index number formula; simplifying it further renders the following equation for the index number:

$$PI_T = \frac{\Sigma_{i=1}^{n}P_{Ti}Q_{0i}}{\Sigma_{i=1}^{n}P_{0i}Q_{0i}} \times 100.$$

For an easier understanding of this formula it can be written in a less mathematical fashion as:

$$PI_T = \frac{\Sigma P_T Q_0}{\Sigma P_0 Q_0} \times 100$$

goods in the market. Hence, inflation is said to occur when most of the prices start rising due to the relative shortage of those goods. Inflation is triggered either by a general increase in the demand for goods and services relative to their supply, or by a general fall in the supply of goods and services relative to their demand. Thus, shortages arising out of too many consumers chasing too few goods result in competition among the consumers, thereby driving the prices up.

## Supply Shock/Cost–Push Inflation

Some of you may recall the formation of the international cartel—Organization of the Petroleum Exporting Countries (OPEC). Little more than a decade after the establishment of OPEC in 1960, prices of crude petroleum shot up steeply due to the Arab oil embargo and later, again, during the Iranian revolution in 1979. The regulation of oil supplies by OPEC and the resultant rise in petroleum prices—from US$3 per barrel in early 1973 to about US$40 per barrel by 1979—led to a major increase in the cost of production in all industries which use petroleum as a crucial source of energy. This led to a sudden supply shock, and the sustained shortage of crude oil thereafter resulted in what is called cost–push inflation. Shortage of crude oil and the resultant high prices of goods which use crude oil in the market result in overall smaller quantities of goods being purchased in the market. This leads to a general reduction in output and employment in the economy. Such an inflation that leads to a lowering of output and employment is known as Stagflation.

In India, this kind of inflation is also brought about by a shortage of agricultural produce due to droughts caused by insufficient rains. Shortage of food and agricultural raw material in relation to the demand leads to a rise in the cost of production and prices in most sectors of the economy. Volumes traded in the market suffer due to high prices.

Inventories mount up, sending a signal to firms to produce less. The result is high prices accompanied by lowered output and employment, in other words, stagflation. And it is not just the supply shock that causes inflation. Prices administered by the government can also be inflationary. For example, with regular frequency, the government offers support prices to farmers for rice, wheat, sugar cane, cotton, and many other cash crops. Of course, these support prices are higher than the free market price. Such price supports increase the cost of production in industries which use agricultural produce as raw material. Overall, therefore, administered prices may result in inflation.

## Demand–Pull Inflation

Inflation can occur even in the absence of supply shocks such as failure of monsoons or a fall in the availability of a critical resource like crude oil. When the demand for goods or services exceeds the existing output levels in the economy, the result is inflation. The cause of an increase in demand could be increased exports, a rise in household and firm spending, increased government purchases, and/or central bank operations.

You must have undoubtedly heard that the real estate prices have rocketed in Bengaluru, Pune, and elsewhere in the country due to the export boom in the information technology (IT) industry in India. With an increased demand for IT services from the developed world, the incomes of IT professionals have gone up substantially, and they have started demanding many goods and services in the market. This has resulted in an increase in realty prices and perhaps a rise in food prices as well. A general rise in prices, however, requires more than just an IT boom. A business-friendly environment nurtured by successive governments in the recent past had made entrepreneurs quite optimistic about the future. As the restrictions on import of technology and capital goods reduced, business enterprises began investing in many projects which had hitherto been considered unprofitable. This optimism resulted in increased investments by firms which, in turn, led to an increased demand for goods and services. Brighter business prospects imply a higher profitability for firms, and this gets reflected in the higher prices of equity/shares in the stock market. And as the wealth of households goes up in the form of high-value shares or equity stocks, they start spending more on goods and services.

Thus, a demand–pull from the external sector and an optimistic reading of the future by firms and households can increase the demand for goods and services relative to the existing output levels, thereby causing inflation in the economy. Certain government and central bank policies of a country can also further add fuel to inflation. For example, the Government of India has embarked upon two key welfare schemes throughout India—the Mahatma Gandhi National Rural Employment Guarantee Scheme (MGNREGS) and the Midday Meal Scheme. Through these schemes, the government spends more than Rs 40,000 crores and Rs 10,000 crores, respectively, every year. Such policies have positive income distributional effects which generate an additional demand for goods and services in the rural areas. Disadvantaged individuals who now earn income through these schemes demand additional food and other commodities in the market. This contributes to inflation. We must note at this time, however, that a small measure of demand–pull inflation is considered good for the economy as it gives an incentive to producers to produce more. And, if the output level rises as a result of a moderate rise in price, inflation stays in check. We will address this particular hypothesis in detail in the next section.

The recent rise in the prices of general commodities— particularly food items—has demonstrated that the growth in output has not kept pace with the rise in prices. If the amount spent on MGNREGS creates additional assets in the form of superior rural roads, wells, bunds, and check dams, this boost in the infrastructure should promote food production and other services in order to keep inflation in check. However, this does not seem to have happened. The fact that, at one time, the Indian government had brought down customs duties on the import of dal and edible oil to zero goes to show that the food output has not kept pace with the growing demand. In fact, recent studies show that almost 40 percent of edible oil was being imported into India. Similarly, in 2010–11, three million tonnes of dal was imported to meet with the domestic shortage. And, as per the India Pulses and Grains Association (IPGA) forecast, the shortage of dal and, hence, its imports will more than double from its existing levels in the next eight years. It is clear that inflationary pressure will not fade away if output levels do not keep pace with the demand.

The most acute form of demand–pull inflation is called hyperinflation. It occurs when the government and the central bank engage in reckless printing of money to make additional payments to various stakeholders. The sequence of events leading to hyperinflation may be as follows: A government owes large amounts to various stakeholders but is unable to finance the payments. It issues new government securities and forces the central bank to buy them in order to generate income. The central bank can buy these securities only by printing new currency. This new currency represents the additional money supply that the central bank generates and makes available to the government to make payments. Such payments made by the government generate income in the hands of people, creating an additional demand in the market, for which no additional output exists. And, ultimately, in order to deal with the increased demand, prices get raised in the market. Various governments and central banks of countries, such as, Germany, Argentina, and a few others, have resorted to this method with devastating effects. At times, inflation rates in these countries have risen higher than 1000 percent per year. The Indian government and the RBI have taken precautions in this respect. In a milder version, the government did monetize its debt in the past, contributing to some inflation in the 1980s. However, this window of ad hoc monetization has been closed by law to the Indian government and RBI since 1994.

## German Hyperinflation: Too Much Money Chasing Too Few Goods!

After the end of the First World War in 1918, Germany was required to make war reparation payments to France and Britain, amounting to hundreds of billions of German marks. Germany was a war-ravaged economy and could not have made arrangements for the reparations immediately. It would either have to default and/or pay for reparations by printing money. To recover the reparations, France captured Ruhr, the industrial province of Germany. Germans workers adopted a method of passive resistance by not working in the factories, though Germany continued to pay their wages. As a result, the printed money that was paid as reparations and the wages for no-work in Ruhr created a demand for goods and services for which there was no corresponding output in the market. The end result was hyperinflation. From 1922 to 1923, the average inflation exceeded 3000 percent. A loaf of bread that cost about 160 marks in 1922 was priced at about 1.5 million marks in September 1923, and it further rose in leaps and bounds by the end of 1923.

This phenomenon of hyperinflation—an extreme form of demand–pull inflation—is captured by an economic postulate called the Quantity Theory of Money. This postulate is popularly described by an equation:

$$M \, V = P \, Y$$

where M is the money supply in the economy (we have defined what is 'money' in an earlier chapter); P is the price level or the index number prevailing in a given period of time; Y is the level of output in the economy; and V is the velocity of money. Velocity of money refers to the average number of times a unit of currency (say, a rupee or a mark) is used in a given period of time. The right-hand side of the equation shows that P times Y (PY) is nothing but the current or nominal GDP as we have defined it in an earlier chapter. If the velocity of money is V, to carry out transactions related to the PY level of GDP, one needs to have M units of money. On an average, each unit of M will be used V times during a given period.

Now, it is easy to see that if $V=\bar{V}$ and $Y=\bar{Y}$ are constants, an increase in money supply M will only lead to an increase in price level P. This is exactly what happened in Germany in the early 1920s. A substantive increase in the money supply to pay for war reparations and wages without production led to a substantive increase in the price level alone, for the output in the economy was held almost constant in relation to the gigantic increases in money supply. This was a classic case of too much money chasing too few goods. Of course, by the end of 1923, the workers were asked go back to work in Ruhr; a new currency, the Reichsmark, was introduced to replace the old German mark; war reparations were rescheduled with more realistic annual targets; and the US government also extended loans to Germany. These measures helped eventually eliminate hyperinflation.

## WHY WORRY ABOUT INFLATION?

Now we know what inflation is, how it is calculated, and what factors may lead to it. However, one simple and practical question we need to clarify is: Why do we worry about inflation? You have heard your grandparents complain that, when they were in their prime, the price of milk was barely 50 paise a litre and that now it is pushing Rs 35 a litre. Of course, it is true that the price of milk has risen many times over, but so has the income of the households over the generations. If prices and income rise in the same proportion, one can continue to consume the same amount of milk as before without any reason to complain. Someone who complains despite both prices and income rising in the same proportion is considered to be suffering from, as economists call it, 'money illusion'. To be fair to grandparents though, they may not be suffering from money illusion since, maybe, their post-retirement monthly pension is not rising in the same proportion!

Similar complaints might come from a college lecturer, an office clerk, or a high-school peon whose salary remains unchanged for years together even as inflation eats into his salary. The complaints arise because, given a fixed income and increasing prices, an individual commands fewer and fewer goods in the marketplace. In this sense, one's real income comes down. Businesses, on the other hand, may not lose as their revenues increase with increasing prices. Thus, inflation results in a redistribution of income that is unfavourable to fixed-income earners. The same can be said of debtors and creditors. Let us consider an individual who borrows a principle amount of Rs 1 lakh in the year 2000 and repays it in the year 2008. If the intervening eight years are marked by high inflation, the principle amount returned in the year 2008 is worth much less in terms of the goods and services that it can buy. Therefore, between debtors and creditors, inflation causes a redistribution of real income in favour of debtors. And, because the real value of cash holdings goes down, one would like to spend before prices rise further, to save less, and to borrow more! As a society, such changes in real income distribution and spending habits are certainly worrisome.

Apart from the above worries, inflation may affect us in still other ways. During inflationary situations, business revenues and profits rise. This sends a signal to firms and investors that business prospects are bright. As a result, investors start buying shares in the stock market, hoping to get high dividends on shares. With the increased demand in the stock market, share prices, too, rise. Those already in possession of shares, see an opportunity to make a profit by selling them. When individuals sell shares at a high price, they make capital gains which are taxable. Part of the rise in share prices may simply be due to the inflationary factor and part may be pure capital gains accruing to the relative high price of the share. Thus, one may need to adjust the total capital gains by removing the inflationary factor. Similarly, while producers may benefit in terms of higher revenues during inflation, they, too, feel the pinch of inflation due to progressive income taxes. In most countries, including India, where governments levy progressive income taxes (see Chapter 2), tax rates rise as incomes rise. Thus, in an inflationary situation, a rise in business revenues puts businesspersons in higher tax brackets, making them pay higher taxes.

Farmers, too, worry about inflation. While the food prices paid by consumers may rise during inflation, farmers claim that the prices they receive are always lower due to a glut in the market during the harvest period. Given that they incur higher costs of production throughout the year due to higher prices of pesticides, seeds, fertilizers, they start claiming higher minimum support prices during the harvest season. Similarly, there may also be demands by agricultural labourers for higher minimum wages during inflation. Therefore, various stakeholders in the economy get affected by inflation. It is for this reason that a pithy statement by Milton Friedman, a recipient of the Nobel Memorial Prize in Economic Sciences, is quoted at the beginning of this chapter, 'Inflation is the one form of taxation that can be imposed without legislation.'

Inflation is also the reason why a comparison of nominal GDP over time becomes meaningless (for GDP, see Chapter 2). Consider the example we used in the first section of this chapter. If GDP consisted of only two goods—food and clothing—the nominal GDP for 2009 would be: (80x5) + (90x2) = Rs 580. In the year 2010, if the prices for these two items rose to Rs 100 and Rs 99, respectively, but there was no change in the quantities produced, then the nominal GDP in 2010 would be: (100x5) + (99x2) = Rs 698. Does the increase in the nominal GDP from Rs 580 to Rs 698 represent any 'real' increase in GDP? Not really, since the output produced did not change at all during the year. How does one find the real GDP for 2010 then? We know from calculations made in the first section of this chapter that, if the price index for the year 2009 is assumed to be 100, the price index for the year 2010 is 120.34. This means an inflation of 20.34 percent. Therefore, to find out the real GDP for 2010, we divide the nominal GDP of 2010 by the inflation factor of 1.2034 (that is, 120.34/100). This give us the real income for 2010 as Rs 698/1.2034 = Rs 580. This income is the same as the one in the previous year which is not surprising, since there was no increase in output in the second year. Hence, the real GDP growth is zero.

Now, instead, if the quantities of food and clothing produced in the year 2010 were 8 and 3, respectively, the growth in real GDP would be 57 percent.[1] Of course, the GDP growth in this particular example is very high for the simple reason that it is an example. But this is how yearly growth rates in GDP are calculated in India. To avoid all such complications of calculation, one might wish, in the first place, that inflation did not take place. However, inflation is inescapable. And, therefore, governments have to calculate the real GDP figures and their growth rates so that these

[1] With quantities of food and clothing produced in 2010 being 8 and 3, respectively, the nominal GDP for 2010 would be Rs 1097. To find the real GDP for 2010, we divide the nominal GDP of 2010 by the inflationary factor of 1.2034, that is, Rs 1097/1.2034 = Rs 912. Rs 912 minus Rs 580 gives a change of Rs 332 in real GDP. The increase of Rs 332 over Rs 580 amounts to a 57 percent increase in real GDP.

statistics become comparable across years and across different countries. By now, you may have decided that inflation is bad and that something must be done about it. True. However, inflation in moderation may do some good as well. It is argued that a little inflation offers an incentive to firms to produce more. To produce more, additional labour is required, leading to greater employment, and there will be more available for society's consumption. Another reason why a little inflation may be practicable relates to the fact that labour is not an inanimate factor of production and that it functions in a manner different from other factors of production. The reasoning is given below.

The forces of demand and supply determine the prices of inputs, namely land, labour, materials, and capital. The prices of non-labour inputs fall when the demand for these inputs decreases in relation to supply. In contrast, however, it is very seldom that wages are adjusted downwards. Workplaces try to avoid such socially unpleasant moves, for labour has both an instrumental value in production and an intrinsic value for itself. But then, businesses are not philanthropic ventures either. How does a business enterprise adjust real wages downwards if the demand for labour is declining in relation to supply? One solution is to keep the nominal wages (that is, money payments) constant while the economy is experiencing a small amount of inflation. In fact, business enterprises may even increase nominal wages to some extent but not at the pace of inflation. That way, nominal wages are not reduced, the unpleasantness associated with such a move is avoided, but the objective of reducing real wages in line with the lower demand for labour is met with. For example, if the inflation rate is, say, 3.5 percent, the nominal wages may be kept constant; or, if they have to be raised, they can be raised less than the full extent of the inflation.

## GETTING THE INFLATION RATE RIGHT

A small amount of inflation may be good; however, in reality, India had been experiencing high inflation for at least a couple of years in the recent past. As per the RBI Annual Report (2011), the price rise in non-administered fuel between January 2011 and July 2011 was about 40 percent. Similarly, the price rise in protein-based food items was as high as 30 percent between January 2010 and June 2010. However, inflation refers to an average general price rise and not a price rise in just one commodity or a group of commodities. This means that one needs to identify the correct basket of goods and services for calculating the price index and the inflation. Moreover, we have also learnt that assigning weights to different groups of commodities is critical since different sets of consumers may lay out different proportions of their spending on different groups of commodities. Therefore, a number of price indices are used to calculate inflation. In fact, you may notice that media and the government keep quoting different inflation rates—namely, inflation-based on consumer price indices, wholesale price indices, and the core and headline inflation.

## Consumer Price Indices (CPIs)

When an aeroplane lands in an Indian city, the cabin crew announces the outside temperature in Celsius. On the other hand, a doctor takes your temperature in Fahrenheit. One uses miles or kilometres to measure distances on land and, for distances at sea or in air, one uses nautilus miles or nautilus kilometres. The choice of a unit of measure is guided by its purpose. Similarly, different price indices are used to describe inflation, the choice being determined by the purpose for which they are used. To measure the cost of living among various segments of Indian population, different CPIs are used. For example, one is for industrial workers CPI(IW); another for agricultural labourers CPI(AL); and yet another for urban non-manual employees. It shouldn't surprise you that the weight assigned to food is 46.2 percent for CPI(IW), and 69.15 percent for CPI(AL). This reflects the fact that food accounts for a much greater share in the total expenditure of agricultural labourers than of industrial workers.

These specific indices are used by governments and firms as reference points to revise pay scales, dearness allowances, and minimum agricultural wages. Over time, some old goods become redundant in the economy and new ones get added. For example, typewriters have become obsolete and many new services have become very common. Hence, the government has to periodically change the basket of commodities used in the calculation of the indices and change the base year as well. For example, from January 2011, the

Indian government has come out with a new set of CPIs—one for the rural population, one for the urban population, and a third one which combines the two. The base year for these CPIs is 2010. It has also widened the scope and coverage of goods and services which capture the changing pattern of consumption of goods and services in India.

## Headline Inflation

You may have come across the term 'headline inflation' in newspapers or on TV news channels. Headline inflation is the inflation which is calculated on the basis of the Wholesale Price Index (WPI), which represents the index of the average price of all commodities at the wholesale level. It excludes prices of services but includes prices of raw materials, semi-finished products, and even imported commodities that are traded at the wholesale level. Therefore, WPI reflects the inflation that is posed to the industrial sector of the economy. A rise in the cost of production ultimately leads to a rise in the retail prices paid by the consumer. Therefore, cost–push inflation is likely to get reflected first in WPI and subsequently in CPI and, hence the name, headline inflation. In WPI, primary and manufactured food articles receive a weight of only 24.31 percent because it includes many more non-food manufactured products accounting for 55 percent. Therefore, it is not surprising that inflation, as measured through WPI, was lower than that measured through CPI, seeing that it was the food prices that had risen significantly over the last two years. For example, the yearly figures of inflation based

129

on WPI and CPI(IW) as reported in January 2011 were 9 percent and 15 percent, respectively. One advantage of WPI is that it is calculated on a weekly basis and is available with a time lag of only two weeks.

## Core Inflation

Agricultural prices are subject to wide fluctuations. That is due to fluctuations in production related to the vagaries of monsoon and the periodic gluts in the market during the peak months of rabi and kharif harvesting. Similarly, fuel prices, too, undergo wide price fluctuations. The international price of crude oil which had been $20 a barrel in 2009, came close to $100 a barrel at the end of 2011. So, fluctuations may not give a correct picture of inflation in the long run. Over a long period of time, such fluctuations may get ironed out. To mitigate their effect, use is made of core inflation, which excludes the prices of food and fuel from the calculation of the price index and the inflation rate. In India, core inflation is calculated by excluding food and fuel prices from WPI. Naturally, one expects that, during rising prices of food and fuel, the core inflation rate would be lower than the headline inflation rate or the one based on CPI. In many countries, core inflation is calculated on the basis of CPI excluding the food and fuel prices. With the wider scope and coverage of goods and services in the new CPIs launched in January 2011, the Government of India may use CPI as the reference index for calculating a representative inflation rate for the country, and for basing the core inflation on CPI without food and fuel prices.

# POLICIES FOR CONTROLLING INFLATION

We have so far discussed what inflation is, how it is calculated, why it occurs, why high inflation is worrisome, and what to make of the different inflation rates based on different indices that are quoted in the media. When prices rise in general and food prices in particular, we observe that all the inflation rates—core inflation, headline inflation, and CPI-based inflation—are high, increasing in that order. For example, in May 2010, the core, the headline, and the CPI(IW) inflation rates were 7.27 percent, 10.6 percent, and 13.9 percent, respectively. If the fuel and food prices were volatile strictly in the short run, RBI would focus on reducing the long-term trend in inflation as given by the core or the headline inflation. However—as has been the case in 2010 and 2011—food and fuel prices kept on increasing steadily over a longer period. Therefore, RBI looked at focusing on reducing all measures of inflation. As for an ideal level of inflation, we have excused 'some' amount of inflation as being good for the economy. The exact figure of 'some' cannot be defined, naturally. Of course, any inflation in double digits or beyond is unacceptable, and even a single-digit inflation figure beyond 5 percent should be a source of worry.

## Easing Supply Constraints

Inflations can occur due to cost–push / supply shock factors, demand–pull factors, or both. Therefore, policies need to be in place for countering both kinds of inflationary pressures. On the supply side, one of the few measures that a government can take to control inflation is easing the supply constraint by removing import restrictions. For example, as reported in *Economic Survey* (Government of India, 2011), on different occasions, the Indian government has brought customs duties down to zero on import of rice, wheat, pulses, crude edible oils, butter, ghee, raw sugar, and onions. This is done in the hope that additional import supplies at cheaper prices would eliminate domestic shortage and reduce prices. As per the RBI Annual Report (2011, p. 24), during 1990–2010, India's population grew at an average rate of 1.8 percent per year and the food grain production grew only at an average rate of 1.6 percent. Therefore, in the long run, investments in agricultural infrastructure and innovative technologies such as genetically modified foods may help ease supply constraint and hence the pressure on prices.

Some calibrations in existing government programmes can also reduce agricultural costs and, in turn, inflation. For example, MGNREGS run by the Government of India spends about Rs 40,000 crores annually on rural employment generation. This scheme was based on the success of the original Employment Guarantee Scheme (EGS) started in Maharashtra in the 1970s. However, deliberately, EGS was never implemented in the busy months of agricultural sowing and harvesting during the kharif and rabi seasons. This prevented labour shortages and wage hikes during agricultural operations. The Union minister of agriculture has now requested that MGNREGS, too, should not be in effect during the busy months of agricultural operations. This will prevent labourers being lured away during the crucial, busy agricultural months. That is how peak-season higher labour costs and the resultant food supply shortages can be avoided. This has the potential to put a downward pressure on inflation. Moreover, unless MGNREGS creates productive assets, such as, all-weather rural roads, wells, and bunds, an increase in the food supply may not be forthcoming.

Another solution to the inflation issue is presenting competition to Agricultural Produce and Marketing Committee (APMC) markets in towns and cities. Allowing private players—including multi-brand retailers who bring in FDI—to deal in retail and wholesale markets will reduce trader margins. An empirical study on domestic and imported apples sold in India shows that there are a number of middlemen in the farm-to-finger supply chain: out of the final rupee spent by a consumer on apples, about 50 percent goes for trader margins. Further, when the cost of production rises, there is a cascading effect on retail price since the middlemen's margins are based on the percentage mark-up on their respective costs. This cascading effect causes inflation in retail prices. More competition through private players will reduce the margins of the middlemen and lower the prices for consumers. Moreover, the modern technology that FDI will introduce in retail will decrease agricultural wastages in the existing multiple distribution stages. Of course, collective decision-making on allowing FDI in retail may take some time but it would put a check on inflation.

## Restricting the Demand–Pull

During an inflationary period, we often read or hear the statement, 'The economy is overheating.' In plain English, this term may be used to signify that something is being overworked or overused. If you drive a car continuously for too long, the engine may overheat. The same holds true for a geyser, especially if it lacks a thermostat. Thus, overheating is associated with the usage of a resource beyond its natural or normal capacity. Examples of overheating in an economy are not very different. There is a term, 'normal employment' of resources. An eight-hour shift in a factory assembly line may be considered normal employment of the assembly line. However, if, for some reason, consumers and firms become optimistic, they may start demanding more goods and services in the market. To satisfy this demand, factory assembly lines may have to be used for a second or even a third shift. Overuse of the factory resource will increase maintenance cost, require overtime payments for workers and, if the demand is still not being met with, factory owners will start looking for other premises, driving up the rental costs. Thus, if an economy enjoys a very positive consumer and business outlook, the demand for goods and services outstrips the capacity constraints or the normal use of the economic resources leading to overheating, that is, an inflationary situation due to excess demand.

Some of the factors that can cause such an optimistic economic outlook are: a strong export demand, innovative practices by firms leading to better business prospects, good governance, or even a return to a riot-free environment. Of course, as we have stated earlier, if this leads to a little inflation and motivates firms to expand capacity and improve technology, the requisite supply would be forthcoming, thereby keeping inflation in check. However, it may take time—and it does take time for productive capacities to expand and new technologies to evolve. In fact, if this does not happen in the short to medium term, inflation becomes a worrying issue. At this stage, governments and central banks intervene, which essentially boils down to reducing the demand for goods and services in the market so that prices are pushed lower.

During inflationary situations, a government would do well to avoid initiating new projects and to hold back on any imminent spending that is in the offing. Else, the additional demand that would get generated due to such policies would add fuel to the fire of inflation. For example, during this high inflationary period, the Indian government may withhold the plan to table the National Food Security Bill in Parliament for its passage will cost the government around Rs 90,000 crores towards subsidized food for the urban and rural poor. Of course, while holding back new initiatives is relatively easy, reducing or rolling back existing spending commitments or increasing taxes to reduce demand puts the government in a tough spot politically. Therefore, quite often the policy focus is placed in RBI's court.

While discussing German hyperinflation, we gathered that printing too much money creates inflation. Conversely, therefore, a reduction in money supply reduces inflation. RBI can reduce the money supply in the economy through different ways. From an earlier chapter on banking, we know that RBI makes it mandatory for commercial banks to maintain the CRR and the SLR. Increasing CRR or SLR by RBI means that banks would have to keep more idle cash as reserve against their deposit liabilities and to invest their funds in government securities, respectively. This reduces the banks' ability to go for multiple deposit and loan creation. With reduced loan facilities, firms can borrow less and, even if they do, it is at a higher rate of interest. Hence, fewer investment projects are viable for firms, thereby, in turn, reducing the demand for plant, machinery, and a host of other goods and services in the market. This lack of demand results in putting a dampening effect on prices.

RBI may alter CRR and SLR, but not frequently. One of the main objectives of these ratios is to avoid a run on banks and to keep at least a part of the depositors' money in secured government bonds. RBI has two other instruments to control the money supply at its disposal—Open Market Operations (OMOs) and altering the repo rate. OMO refers to the buying and selling of government securities by RBI in the market. When RBI sells government securities in the market, banks and financial institutions buy them and money flows from the private sector to RBI, resulting in lowering the deposit amounts in commercial banks. This reduces the cash in banks which is needed to create multiple deposits and to extend loans. Hence, through the multiplier effect, the ability of banks to give loans comes down. Once again, loans become scarce and interest rates rise, leading to fewer investments by firms. This reduces the demand for goods and services in the market, adversely affecting prices.

The repo rate refers to the 're-purchase order' rate that is available to commercial banks under RBI's Liquidity Adjustment Facility (LAF). Repo is RBI's most talked-about instrument in newspapers and TV news. For example, during the years 2010 and 2011, RBI increased the repo rate more than a dozen times. At present, this rate hovers around 8.25 percent. To understand why RBI changes the repo rate frequently, we need to understand LAF. Through LAF, commercial banks can secure short-term funds by selling government securities to RBI for on-lending to customers, meeting with their daily/overnight requirements of CRR, SLR or meet any other financial obligations. However, LAF mandates that banks must repurchase the same securities at a later date. The securities are repurchased by the banks at a price higher than their selling price. Essentially, the difference in the two prices expressed as an annualized percentage of the selling price is the repo rate. Thus, the repo rate is nothing but the short-term interest rate at which commercial banks borrow from RBI. If the repo rate is increased, it becomes costlier for commercial banks to borrow from RBI. In turn, banks would also give loans to private firms at a higher interest rate. At a higher interest rate, a smaller number of investment projects become viable for the private sector. This

## Isaac Newton, Forged Currency, and Controlling Inflation

Most people know that Isaac Newton was a great scientist and mathematician who discovered gravity, the laws of motion, and calculus. However, what they don't know is that Newton also controlled the supply of money in the United Kingdom! Circa 1696, Newton was the Warden of the Royal Mint in UK. In those days, one in every four coins was a fake, half the gold coins had bits clipped off them, and the clipped bits were being sold for profit. With the increased supply of (forged) money, the result would have been inflation. In fact, other countries started refusing to accept English coins. The scientist in Newton could not sit quiet. As Warden of the Mint, he designed and installed new minting machines that were eight times faster than the previous ones, and the coins were harder to forge or clip. The law in those days also allowed Newton to reward anyone who gave information about forgers and, if an arrested forger informed about two other forgers, he/she got let off. Not surprisingly, people started talking, and Newton went after William Chaloner, a forger and high-society man. Chaloner was eventually hanged for his crime and Newton had a good control over the money supply and, perhaps, on inflation.

History repeats itself. The RBI Annual Report (2011, p. 125) shows that a total of 435,607 pieces of forged bank notes were detected in the year 2010–11. This is an increase of about 9 percent over the earlier two years. The actual number perhaps is quite large, for these notes are just what they are—the detected ones. Currently, India depends entirely on foreign countries for procuring the critical paper, ink and other security features of the notes. If one is to go by the reports in rediff.com, the forged currency is allegedly pumped into India by foreign intelligence agencies through their operatives in the neighbouring countries. It should not come as a surprise that, while the Indian rupee was readily accepted in Nepal for decades, high-denomination notes are not accepted there anymore. Perhaps, the volume of forged currency may or may not be large enough to cause inflation. However, the danger is very much there. Therefore, with a view to indigenizing the production of paper, ink and other raw materials required for the currency notes, a paper mill is being set up in Mysore. The mill is a joint venture between Bharatiya Reserve Bank Note Mudran Private Limited (BRBNMPL) and Security Printing & Minting Corporation of India Limited (SPMCIL). The mill will have a production capacity of 6000 metric tonnes of currency paper.

causes the demand for investment goods to fall and, thereby, stall inflation.

In this chapter, we have focused on the anatomy of inflation. While concluding the chapter we explain that demand–pull inflation may lead to overheating of the economy, that is, utilization of resources beyond their normal capacity. If resources get overworked, but a corresponding capacity expansion does not take place relative to the demand, inflation occurs. However, markets experience both boom and bust. A reverse phenomenon may also occur, with an under-utilization of resources as the result of a lack of demand for goods and services. This phenomenon, described by the term 'recession', will be taken up for discussion in the next chapter.

## REFERENCES:

Deodhar, S., Landes, M. and Krissoff, B., (2006), 'Prospects for India's Emerging Apple Market', Electronic Output Report from ERS, USDA, FTS-319-01. Accessed on September 9, 2012, http://www. ers.usda.gov /publications/fts/jan06/ fts31901/ fts31901.pdf

Government of India, (2011), *Economic Survey*, 2010–11, Ministry of Finance, Government of India (GOI), February, New Delhi: Oxford University Press

Poskitt, K., (1999), *Dead Famous: Isaac Newton and His Apple*, London: Scholastic

Reserve Bank of India, (2011), 'Reserve Bank of India Annual Report 2010–11,' http://rbi.org.in/scripts/publications.aspx? publication=Annual

# READY RECKONER

**Base year:** In the context of price indices, this refers to the year for which the price level is assumed to be 100.

**Consumer Price Index (CPI):** CPI represents the index of the average price of all goods and services traded at the retail level. Specific to the purpose, different CPIs are calculated, such as, for industrial workers, agricultural labourers, and urban, non-manual employees.

**Core inflation:** Inflation in the economy, measured on the basis of the WPI without considering food and fuel prices.

**Headline inflation:** Inflation in the Indian economy measured on the basis of the Wholesale Price Index.

**Inflation:** A sustained, general rise in the price level.

**Laspeyres Price Index:** A price index representing a weighted average of the prices of different goods or group of goods, where the weights are decided on the basis of the share of the good or the group of goods in the total expenditure in the base year.

**Open Market Operations (OMO):** The selling (or buying) of government securities by the central bank of a country to (and from) commercial banks, financial institutions, and/or others in the financial market.

**Price index:** Represents a weighted average of the prices of different goods and services or group of goods and services. The weights are determined on the basis of the share of the good or a group of goods in the total expenditure.

**Real GDP:** The Nominal GDP divided by the inflation factor.

**Repo rate:** The rate at which commercial banks borrow short-term funds from the Reserve Bank of India.

**Wholesale Price Index (WPI):** Represents the index of the average price of all commodities at the wholesale level, which includes the prices of raw materials, semi-finished products, and even imported commodities that are traded at the wholesale level, but excludes the prices of services.

# CHAPTER 6

# THE BOOM AND BUST PHENOMENA

*'Everything in the world may be endured except continued prosperity.'*

—JOHANN VON GOETHE

## BUSINESS CYCLE

Free market economies go through what is termed a business cycle. For example, the period during the three fiscal years, 2005–06 to 2007–08 witnessed a stellar performance by the Indian economy, where the average GDP growth rate was 9.47 percent. And then, all of a sudden, the GDP growth rate dipped to 4.93 percent in 2008–09. While the fortunes of the economy revived a while later, prospects for 2012–13, going by the media reports, did not look that good, either. In fact, episodes of such booms and busts with uncertain periodicity get repeated. The corroboration of this is shown in Figure 6.1 which shows the GDP growth rates for India from the fiscal year 1966–67 to the fiscal year 2011–12. The GDP growth rates show troughs and peaks over time. Let us pinpoint some major socio-economic and/or political events that have preceded or coincided with most of the troughs.

The negative growth rate of about -0.04 percent in 1966–67 was preceded by the war with Pakistan on the western front. The very low growth rate of about 1.63 percent in 1971–72 and the negative growth rate of about -0.55 percent in 1972–73 can be attributed to the war that carved out a new nation—Bangladesh. War creates uncertainty and fear which makes businessmen wary of future prospects and makes them hold back on new investment plans. This lowers the demand for investment goods in the market. Consumers, too, defer any major purchases of consumer durables and real estate. This leads to a lowering of demand and an accumulation of inventories, which sends a signal to businesses that they should produce less which, in turn, leads to a negative GDP growth rate. Of course, war-related expenses increase the demand for some goods such as arms and ammunition, which however, add virtually nothing to the final goods and services consumed by households.

The biggest trough in the GDP growth rates appears in the fiscal year 1979–80—the year of the oil shock when the world experienced a shortage of crude oil due to the Iranian revolution and successive price hikes by OPEC. GDP fell by a whopping 5.24 percent during that year. Another monumental event that affected the economy was the beginning of economic reforms in India in 1991. Prospects were very bleak for the economy at that time—businesses refrained from major decisions in the expectation of a devaluation of the Indian rupee. As was feared, the rupee was devalued by about 20 percent in July 1991. The GDP growth rate came down to barely 1 percent that year. And, a decade later, the World Trade Centre bombing on September 11, 2001 jolted the economic world. Air travel and global trade were substantially reduced in the wake of the event, bringing the GDP growth rate in 2002 down to 3.77 percent. The last full downturn in India was witnessed in 2008, immediately following the 2007 subprime crisis in the US, which caused a severe downturn and sharp fall in the US GDP by 2.67 percent.

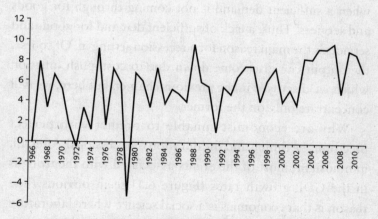

**Figure 6.1: India's Annual GDP Growth Rates
(1966–67 to 2011–12)**

Source: *World Bank and Organisation for Economic Co-operation and Development (OECD) national accounts data files. The data for 2011–12 is a projection*

145

In economics, the downturn of an economy—expressed by a negative GDP growth rate—is known as recession. A more technical, textbook definition defines recession as a phenomenon where the GDP falls (that is, the GDP growth rate is negative) at least for two consecutive quarters. Now, India has not experienced a negative GDP growth rate since 1979, but, significant dips in the GDP growth rates can also be defined as recession. A negative GDP growth rate or a sharp fall in the GDP growth rate indicates a lowered output of goods and services in several, if not all, industries. One of the reasons behind the reduced output is caution exercised by firms due to accumulation of inventories. Inventories pile up when a sufficient demand is not coming through for goods and services. Thus, a lack of sufficient demand for goods and services is the main reason for a recession setting in. Of course, the output can also come down due to cost–push inflation which we discussed in the previous chapter, but here, we will concentrate only on the former.

Why are economists unable to predict with perfect precision the timing and the duration of recessions? After all, in hindsight, most of the events associated with the troughs in the GDP growth rates (Figure 6.1) seem obvious. The reason is that economics is a social science where laboratory experiments are not possible. For example, we know with certainty that under controlled conditions, two units of hydrogen (H) and one unit of oxygen (O) produce water ($H_2O$). In an economy, there are thousands of variables and events at work, simultaneously and independently. Therefore, predictions have to be based on assumptions about certain variables and events. And, given the enormity of the complex market forces, economists do a reasonably good job given the paucity of information. In fact, even in physical sciences many things are not certain—aren't we taught the cardinal principle that light travels in a straight line, only to be told later that, under some other conditions, it may not? Or that, while some assumptions explain light as a particle, some others explain it as a wave!

Of course, some events are more predictable that others. While the timing and duration of wars may be difficult to predict, the likely consequences of the formation of the OPEC cartel or of the events leading up to the devaluation of the Indian rupee in 1991 were predictable enough, though not necessarily avoidable. The actions that led to the subprime crisis (we will discuss this later) might possibly have remained 'insider information' till the crisis broke out, thereby eluding the economists. The government of Greece had borrowed heavily over the years and, by 2010, its debt exceeded much more than 100 percent of GDP. Only now has the world come to know that the debt crisis in Greece was partly due to fiscal deficits being under-reported. Moreover, one is generally quite unaware of how inefficient or otherwise newly elected governments may be in undertaking their legislative, executive, and judicial duties. However, one thing is clear—negative events such as the one mentioned here create a sense of pessimism among firms and consumers. Keynes argued that 'animal spirits' are dimmed by such events which lead

## Dimmed Animal Spirits and the Recession

An article in the *Business Standard* of December 21, 2011 reported that India's largest domestic airline, Jet Airways, had told its 3000-strong cabin crew to take a one-day's leave without pay each month. A senior executive at Jet Airways was quoted as saying that yields were not going up and Jet had had to put a freeze on all capital expenditures, which include ground support equipment, information technology, even furniture. And, ten days prior to this news, Shekhar Gupta, the Editor-in-Chief of the *Indian Express,* wrote in his column that blank hoardings staring at us on the busy drive between Sahar airport and Mumbai city signify a sinking feeling—recession is coming. Kaushik Basu, economist and chief economic adviser to the Indian government, said in an interview with *India Today* (November 21, 2011) that he was unhappy about the delay in the implementation of the GST which would give a boost to growth.

Keynes had summed up the above scenarios by saying that positive activities of businesses depend on spontaneous optimism and an urge to action which he called 'animal spirits'. He used this colourful term to describe one of the essential ingredients for economic prosperity—confidence. According to him, animal spirits are a particular sort of confidence, a naïve optimism. To paraphrase Keynes (1936, pp. 161–62), when economic calculations are supported by animal spirits, the thought of making losses is put aside, just as a healthy man puts aside the expectation of death. And, importantly, this is substantially dependent on the socio-economic and political environment which should be congenial to the business community. If the environment is such that animal spirits are dimmed, the enterprise may fade. It is the uncertain environment that weakens the state of confidence to which practical men always pay the closest and most anxious attention.

The action taken by Jet Airways and the observations made by Shekhar Gupta and Kaushik Basu suggest that animal spirits were dimmed and confidence weakened at the end of the calendar year 2011. The socio-economic and political environment was vitiated by various alleged big-ticket corruption scams such as the 2G spectrum, the Radia phone-tapping episode, and the hasty introduction and withdrawal of the bill to allow multi-brand FDI in the retail sector. In fact, Gupta mentions that corporates are moving investments abroad, and Basu considered it as worrisome if this happens to escape bureaucratic hurdles. What they seem to hint at is that while foreign investors may wait and watch due to uncertain FDI policies, importantly, Indian capitalists also seem to be discouraged to invest in India. Various scams, inordinate delays in decision-making, and bureaucratic hurdles in setting up industries seem to make foreign destinations much more attractive to Indian businessmen. Moreover, since the US and Europe are still recovering from recession, demand for India's exports too was not likely to pick up soon.

A few of the important tasks for the government, therefore, is to engage in a dialogue with industry to reassure, provide good governance, create a congenial environment, and foster business confidence. In short, promote the proverbial animal spirits.

to a lowering of demand for goods and services, ultimately leading to a recession.

## THE BOTTOM LINE: UNEMPLOYMENT RATE

Why do we worry so much about the boom and the bust phases? Well, during the boom period, the demand for goods and services in the marketplace is high and on the rise, and it is reflected in the high growth rates of GDP. This is good news for the economy, because a higher GDP and a higher output mean that there is more employment in the economy—more employment of factors of production in general, and of labour in particular. Should the target of the government or industry then be a zero unemployment rate? Before we address this issue, we need to understand unemployment better. A person is considered involuntarily unemployed if he/she is looking for work at the going wage but does not find one. By analogy, someone who is voluntarily not working at the given market wage is not part of the labour force. Similarly, individuals, who are students, or perform only domestic duties, are too young or too old, or live on alms, are not part of the workforce. Therefore, a workforce consists of those who are employed and those who are involuntarily unemployed. The unemployment rate is defined as a percentage of the workforce that is involuntarily unemployed.

So, to come back to our question—should the government or industry aim for a zero unemployment rate? A simplistic view would suggest yes, but pragmatic and economic reasoning argues that this is not possible. You will notice that many people might be between jobs. They may have quit one job and be on the lookout for a better opportunity. Similarly, students who have recently graduated would not necessarily find jobs immediately. This kind of unemployment is referred to as 'frictional' unemployment. Moreover, although the total number of jobs available may not change, the job requirements might change due to shifting importance within different industries. Thus, individuals may stay out of work due to a temporary mismatch between job requirements and individual skill sets. For example, if the demand for civil engineers is going down but the software industry is on the lookout for qualified programmers, an unemployed civil engineer may retrain himself/herself by doing some computer courses and seek employment in the software industry. This out-of-work retraining period is described as 'structural' unemployment. It follows that frictional and structural unemployment will always remain in an economy. Therefore, the unemployment rate associated with these two types of unemployment is described as the 'natural rate' of unemployment or the level of unemployment associated with full-employment of resources. A rule of thumb in the Western world is that 4 to 5 percent unemployment is natural and consistent with full-employment of resources.

While discussing demand–pull inflation in the previous chapter we had addressed the issue of economy overheating— that is, when the demand for goods and services keeps increasing (a rise in animal spirits at play), inventories may go down, prices may rise, and firms will try to produce more.

This forces firms to overwork the factors of production. This applies to labour as well. During the upswing of the business cycle, the unemployment rate may temporarily go below the natural rate. In fact, the labour turnover is very high during such periods as people move from job to job looking for better prospects—quits are pro-cyclical. However, this cannot be sustained for long and eventually rapid inflation may result. In the long run, production capacities may expand, technology may improve, and therefore, inflation may come down. However, one cannot sit back and watch the inflation rise, for, as we have discussed in the previous chapter, inflation creates its own set of problems. There, we also addressed the policies which the government and RBI may adopt to curtail such demand–pull inflation.

On the other hand, it may also happen that animal spirits get dimmed and confidence levels are lowered because of a variety of socio-economic and political causes. This represents the downswing of the business cycle—the bust phenomenon. In such a situation, the demand for goods and services falls and causes the unemployment rate to increase far beyond the natural rate of unemployment. This happens because, when the demand for goods and services is down, and firms accumulate inventories, they receive a signal that demand is low, and then, they plan to produce less. If they produce less, lower amounts of factors of production, including labour, are required. This kind of unemployment—that goes well beyond the natural rate of unemployment, and is associated with a business downturn—is called 'cyclical' unemployment.

Thus, if (job) quits are pro-cyclical, (job) firing is counter-cyclical occurring on the downturn of the business cycle. If we extend this analogy to the education sector, you will notice that the demand for higher education seems to be counter-cyclical. When graduates lose jobs in a recessionary period, the opportunity cost of their time is low and they go for skill-enhancement through higher education. On the other hand, if the economy is doing very well, graduates easily find employment, and they even quit their current jobs for better-paying ones. In such a situation, the opportunity cost of going for higher education is very high. This, perhaps, explains why applications for PhD programmes seem counter-cyclical!

If the booms and the busts are organically associated with the livelihood of the people, governments must know the extent and the direction of change of unemployment rates. For example, in the year 2009, the US unemployment rate had gone above 10 percent. However, with the timely activation of economic policies it came down, though not significantly, to 8.6 percent in November 2011. In India, it is difficult to know unemployment rate on a regular basis, for the National Sample Survey Office (NSSO) conducts employment surveys once in five years (see box below). Nonetheless, the criticality of measuring unemployment is not lost on the government, since a high incidence of unemployment not only leads to a lower output but also has the potential for a rise in crime and social unrest. As was referred to in Chapter 1, Medley of Government and Private Sector, unemployment seems to create a negative externality on society, and government intervention is called for in terms of what is called the fiscal policy of the government and the monetary policy of RBI.

## FISCAL AND MONETARY POLICIES

Radical free traders argue that governments need not intervene in the market to check the boom and the bust phase. They believe that markets will revert to full employment of resources through changes in prices and wages. However, many economists, including Keynes, argue that, if a lack of demand and dimmed animal spirits lead an economy to operate at high unemployment rates, and it continues to stay that way, then—and perhaps only in the long run—prices and wages could adjust themselves to reach full employment of labour once again. However, people do not have the patience to wait long enough for self-correction by market forces. Keynes is famously quoted as saying, 'In the long run we are all dead.' That is, if unemployment is high, then it is critical we do something about it in the short run itself. Fiscal and monetary policies of the government are, therefore, short-run remedies to bring the economy back to the full-employment level of GDP—a GDP that is consistent with the natural rate of unemployment.

### *Fiscal Policy*

A recession that occurs due to a fall in the demand for goods and services is characterized by a fall in GDP (or a sharp fall in the GDP growth rate) and high unemployment. In such a situation, the government follows what is called

## Unemployment Rate in India: Who Knows?

Referring to the rustling papers in their hands and tick-marking with a pen as they speak, newsreaders on Indian TV channels throw rapid-fire economic statistics at us with élan. The routine statistics include the stock market indices and headline inflation rates. GDP growth rates are also shared, although less frequently. However, India's unemployment rates are hardly quoted. In contrast, on American TV, the US unemployment rates get quoted every month. For example, while the unemployment rate in October 2009 was 10.2 percent, over time it came down to 8.2 percent by March 2012. This corresponds to a fall in unemployment from 15.7 million people to 12.7 million people respectively. The monthly trends over the years indicate that the unemployment rate is declining in the US. The US Bureau of Labor Statistics has been calculating the US monthly unemployment rates since 1940. Every month, 60,000 households numbering about 110,000 individuals are sampled to elicit their activity status in the reference week of the month. One-fourth of the households are changed every month to avoid repetition. Based on their responses, individuals are classified as employed, unemployed and out-of-the-labour-force. A person is considered employed if he/she has done any work at all for pay or profit during the survey week.

In contrast, Indian data becomes available only every five years. The NSSO conducted its latest (sixty-sixth) round of survey from July 2009 to June 2010. In all, 100,957 households were interviewed through a stratified sample. The data is collected using three approaches: Usual Principle Status (UPS); Current Weekly Status (CWS); and Current Daily Status (CDS). UPS relates to the activity status (employed, unemployed, or out-of-the-labour-force) of a person during the reference period of 365 days preceding the date of survey. The status in which a person spent a relatively longer time is used to decide UPS. CWS is obtained for a person during a reference period of seven days preceding the date of survey. A person is considered as a worker if he/she has performed any economic activity at least for one hour on any day of the reference week. For CDS, a person is considered as working (employed) for a full day if he/she worked for four hours or more during each day of the reference week.

Of the three rates, UPS is the most liberal, followed by CWS and CDS. Expectedly, NSSO unemployment rates were 2.5 percent, 3.6 percent, and 6.6 percent for UPS, CWS, and CDS, respectively. The CWS rate of 3.6 percent is comparable in terms of definition with that of the US rate. However, all the three rates appear very low indeed! Interestingly, the Ministry of Labour and Employment (MOL&E) intends to conduct employment surveys every year. Recently, it conducted its very first survey for the period 1-4-2009 to 31-3-2010. Using a similar stratified sampling method for 46,000 households, it measured the unemployment rate for India using UPS. The UPS unemployment rate with which it came up was quite high at 9.4 percent! For women, it was 14.6 percent. Given that the estimates of UPS rates are very liberal, one would expect the CWS and the CDS rates to be much higher. At the start of 2010, to bring out reliable estimates of unemployment rates on a regular basis, the government-appointed Committee on Periodic Labour Force Survey suggested a fine-tuned methodology to conduct quarterly surveys. Hopefully, publication of reliable, quarterly (if not monthly) unemployment rates will give a quicker realization of the impact of the boom and bust cycles in India.

an expansionary fiscal policy. This involves increasing government spending and/or cutting taxes. Essentially, the government tries to give a fillip to the demand for goods and services which has come down due to recession. The expansionary fiscal policy is a very potent tool, because, an increase in spending or a cut in taxes does not increase GDP only by the amount of the expenditure or the tax cut, but in multiples of it. Let us see below how this happens.

Let us suppose that the government hires people by paying them Rs 100 for constructing a dam. Assuming that people save 30 percent of their income, they will spend Rs 70 on purchasing goods and services. This expenditure of Rs 70 becomes an income for some other individuals, like, grocers and tailors. They, too, will save 30 percent of this amount and spend Rs 49. This chain of spending increases GDP in successive rounds by Rs 100, Rs 70, Rs 49, and so on. In all, the addition of this geometric series amounts to Rs 333.33. Thus, the original employment of workers, by spending Rs 100, generates employment in many other sectors, and the total addition to GDP turns out to be 3.33

times the original spending. This 3.33 is called the 'income multiplier'. Now, let us consider the possibility of a tax reduction by the government. A reduction of tax by Rs 100 causes people to spend Rs 70 in the first round. This spending of Rs 70 becomes an income for others and they, too, will save 30 percent of this amount (Rs 21) and spend Rs 49. Thus, when taxes are cut, income generation in successive rounds is by Rs 70, Rs 49, Rs 34.3, and so on. In all, the addition of this geometric series amounts to Rs 233.33, that is, 2.33 times the original reduction of Rs 100 in taxes. The income expansion through a tax cut is lower by Rs 100, for the government itself does not spend Rs 100 in the very first round. However, it is clear that an expansionary fiscal policy raises GDP in multiples of the original spending or of the tax cut.

We see a real-life example of this in India in the recent past. If you recall from Chapter 2 on Budget, Deficits and Taxation, the fiscal deficit for the Central government in India was 2.5 percent in the year 2007–08. The GDP growth rate that year was 9.82 percent. However, the very next year, the GDP growth rate fell to 4.93 percent. This sudden fall was triggered by the subprime crisis in the US which resulted in a recession (see box below). There was no way that the Indian government could have remained a mere spectator to this development. In addition to its fiscal spending on the MGNREGS, highway projects, and Sixth Pay Commission disbursements, importantly, over time, it reduced excise duties from a high of about 14 percent to

8 percent. Service tax, too, was cut from 12 percent to 10 percent. Naturally, this expansionary fiscal policy resulted in a fiscal deficit amounting to 6 percent and 6.3 percent in the next two years, 2008–09 and 2009–10 respectively. But it had a salutary effect on growth: the GDP growth rate bounced back, averaging about 9 percent during the fiscal years 2009–10 and 2010–11.

Expansionary fiscal policy was a revolutionary idea which Keynes propounded for reducing unemployment—a deficient demand in a recessionary period could be countered by an increase in government spending or by tax cuts which increase demand in multiples of the initial spending or of the tax cut. However, there are limits to how much the government can spend and how much taxes it can cut, for it could snowball into high fiscal deficits. In Chapter 2 on Budget, Deficits and Taxation, we did figure out that high fiscal deficits cause a crowding-out of private investments, and may increase the trade deficit as well. Accumulated fiscal deficits could lead governments to high indebtedness. The European PIIGS (Portugal, Italy, Ireland, Greece, and Spain) countries today are having a hard time repaying their debts. As per IMF statistics, Greece's public debt had crossed 142 percent in 2010. Its inability to repay is causing enormous economic hardship to the country and the rest of the world. Moreover, while it may be easier for governments to start incurring certain expenditures during recession, it is politically not easy to withdraw spending when the economy is booming. Therefore, demand management policies cannot be exclusively dependent on fiscal policies alone. RBI, India's central bank, also has an important role to play in preventing the extremities of the boom and the bust through its own independent policies of demand management.

## Monetary Policy

In earlier chapters we acquainted ourselves with how governments began to mint and print money. We also understood that an unbridled use of the central bank by a government to augment the money supply and to finance its expenditures can lead to hyperinflation. Over the decades, however, governments have accorded an independent and responsible role to their central banks. India is no exception to it. Today, RBI follows an independent monetary policy to control inflation and to boost demand during recessionary periods. In the previous chapter, we discussed the instruments that it uses to control inflation. While we did not formally christen the policy then, RBI's stance for controlling the demand–pull inflation that typically occurs when the economy is overheated during a boom period is called the 'contractionary monetary policy'.

On the other hand, if the economy is in recession due to a deficient demand for goods and services, RBI may engage in an expansionary monetary policy. We know that recession is associated with high cyclical unemployment. Therefore, to increase employment, RBI has to induce firms in some way to start new investment projects. New investment projects would be taken up if the cost of capital for the firms were to come down. This means that the interest rates in the economy must come down. RBI can reduce the interest rates if a larger supply of loans is forthcoming—it may then put downward pressure on the interest rates. We know from our discussion in previous chapters that an increased availability of loans in the banking system happens through an increase in the money supply in the economy. How can RBI ensure that the money supply, and therefore, the supply of loans, is augmented in the economy? There are a few ways in which it can do so.

RBI can decrease the CRR or the SLR so that banks are left with more cash on hand per deposit received. This would enable banks to initiate multiple credit/deposit creation (see Chapter 3). This would lead to a bigger money supply and an increased availability of loans in the market, thereby exerting a downward pressure on the interest rates. Similarly, RBI may engage in an OMO to buy government securities from the market. When RBI buys the securities, it is tantamount to cash or money flowing into the private sector which would get deposited in bank accounts. This would increase the cash on hand with banks with which they would be able to initiate multiple credit/deposit creation. Once again, this would amount to an increased money supply and an increased availability of loans in the market which would exert a downward pressure on interest rates.

There is another way to look at OMO operations. When RBI decides to purchase government securities from the market, the demand for government securities goes up. This raises the price of government securities. Let us suppose that the initial price of a security was Rs 100 and that one got 10 percent interest on this original value of the security. This means that Rs 10 is paid every period as interest. Now, assume that the security price goes up in the market to Rs 120 as a result of OMO-buying by RBI. This means that now, any new buyer of government securities, would get Rs 10 from the government (10 percent on the original value of Rs 100) on a security which he/she would buy for Rs 120. The earning of Rs 10 over the purchase price of Rs 120 implies that now, the new interest rate is [10/120] x 100, amounting to 8.33 percent. Thus, an OMO-purchase of government securities by RBI leads to a fall in the market interest rate.

For about a decade now, RBI has created a new and popular window for commercial banks to borrow from RBI. As referenced in the previous chapter, this is called the LAF. Commercial banks generally need funds for short-term purposes to on-lend to its customers, maintain CRR, SLR requirements, or fund any other temporary obligations. To facilitate this, RBI enters into an agreement with commercial banks, whereby the latter sell government securities to RBI and simultaneously place a repurchase order (Repo) with it for the same securities for a future date. The repurchase price is higher than the selling price. This effectively means that commercial banks borrow temporary funds from RBI. The difference in price—expressed as an annualized percentage of the selling price—represents the interest rate and is popularly known as the 'repo rate'. The repo rate has been effectively

## US Subprime Crisis Exported to India!

We have been making references to subprime crisis at a few places in this chapter. While the prime lending refers to the loans offered to the most creditworthy customers, subprime lending refers to the loans given to borrowers who do not have good credit history and may have unstable or low incomes. Banks generally give loans to such subprime customers at a higher interest rate. However, the US interest rates were quite low during 2001 to 2005, and, in the eagerness to sell homes and to offer credit, loans were granted to many subprime US borrowers. Since real estate prices were high, banks and customers used the very homes they were buying as collateral against the loans. These subprime loan assets were sold by banks to government-sponsored enterprises (GSE) such as Fannie Mae and Freddie Mac. The GSEs in turn repackaged these loans as mortgage-backed securities (MBS) with a much higher credit rating. Foreign investors readily bought these MBS.

Over time, however, housing bubble burst, real estate prices started going down and interest rates went up. By the third quarter of 2007, it had become clear that subprime borrowers were defaulting on loan payments. As home prices had also come down, now loans could not be recovered through foreclosures. The ultimate buyers of MBS got wind of it and started selling MBS in the US stock market. Panic gripped the market and stock prices plunged. Lehman Brothers, a leading financial firm, went bankrupt in September 2008. Now the proverbial 'animal spirits' dimmed. Many existing investment projects were wound up and prospective ones shelved which resulted in a recession in the US. To recover financial losses in the US, investors started liquidating overseas portfolio investments including those in India. Therefore, stock prices plummeted in India as well. As investors took funds out of India, increased demand for US dollar resulted in depreciation of rupee making exports difficult. Moreover, India's exports further dwindled because of the recession in the US and Europe. Thus, falling exports and falling stock prices dimmed the business confidence in India, and production and investments fell. The recession had been passed on to India. The result—the GDP growth dropped to 4.93 percent in 2008–09.

To counter this, the Indian government adopted an expansionary fiscal policy by cutting excise duty to 8 percent and service tax to 10 percent. RBI too followed expansionary monetary policy by lowering the repo rate significantly to give boost to domestic investment projects. And, lo and behold! The economy bounced back in the next two years (2009–10, 2010–11) with an average GDP growth rate of about 9 percent.

used by RBI as a monetary policy tool. Lower the repo rate, higher will be the expansion in money supply and availability of loans. For example, in the aftermath of the subprime crisis, at one stage RBI lowered the repo rate all the way down to 4.75 percent, a far cry from 8.5 percent, the rate that existed in December 2011.

Monetary policy, therefore, can be summarized as the management of market interest rates, changing the stock of money supply in the economy, and changing the availability of credit in the market. You may notice that the media uses various terms to describe RBI's monetary policy stance. For example, if it is following the expansionary monetary policy, some news items may say, 'RBI has engaged in quantitative easing'; others may describe the policy by saying, 'RBI is pumping liquidity into the market.' It all boils down to increasing the money supply and the credit availability, and lowering the interest rates, all of which promote the undertaking of more investment projects. And the ultimate objective, through this, is to increase the GDP growth rate and reduce unemployment.

## A RECENT EPISODE: STAGFLATION

Throughout this chapter we have presented the stylized facts of the business cycle and the remedies to dampen it. For example, owing to some negative socio-economic and political factors, business pessimism sets in, and a deficient demand leads to recession. This results in a fall in GDP or in the GDP growth rate, and higher unemployment. A price rise is not a concern in a recession which is caused by deficient demand. In fact, prices may go down. In such a situation, expansionary fiscal and monetary policies are adopted to revive the economy. On the other hand, if the economy is overheated, that is, there is a high growth rate in GDP, a low unemployment rate (perhaps lower than the natural rate), and high inflation, the contractionary fiscal and monetary policy will be followed.

In the aftermath of the subprime crisis, economies the world over suffered a recession, which in the US and the

UK turned almost into a depression, that is, a very severe form of recession. India's GDP growth rate suddenly fell from 9.82 in the fiscal year 2007–08 to 4.93 in the fiscal year 2008–09, but it pulled out of this recession through the stylized expansionary fiscal and monetary policies. As a result, in the fiscal years 2009–10 and 2010–11, the GDP growth once again averaged about 9 percent. At the beginning of this chapter, we quoted a statement by the German philosopher Johann von Goethe: 'Everything in the world may be endured except continued prosperity.' This statement best summarizes the discussion in this chapter. Just when everyone had thought that India was once again cruising at a 9+ GDP growth rate, double-digit inflation surfaced in the economy. Food and fuel inflation continued throughout 2011. Moreover, financial crises surfaced in many European countries around May 2010 dampening stock-market activity and international trade. And, to add to this, business confidence was weakened due to successive corruption allegations and scams such as the 2G spectrum. Very slow progress on many of the fiscal reform promises also contributed to this loss of confidence.

The sum total of the above developments was that, on the one hand, cost–push inflation raised its head, and on the other, a deficient demand in the economy slowed down the GDP growth rate. This meant that India in 2011 was suffering from stagflation, that is, the simultaneous existence of inflation and unemployment. Double-digit inflation was such a major concern that RBI throughout the year increased the repo rate more than a dozen times in the hope that private spending would get halted due to the hike in the interest rate and inflation would be curtailed. But this meant that the GDP growth rate would go down. It is now confirmed that the GDP growth rate did come down by at least about 2 percentage points in the fiscal year 2011–12. The saving grace is that because India's GDP had been growing at a high rate, the 2 percent drop still meant that GDP grew at about 7 percent.

Handling stagflation—promoting GDP growth and reducing inflation—is always difficult. The stylized fiscal and monetary policies offer a trade-off between the two. Either they extinguish inflation at the cost of growth or have growth at the cost of inflation. Therefore, the stylized fiscal and monetary policies have to be complemented by some tailor-made policies in right earnest. These policies should achieve two things: ease the supply constraints, particularly in agriculture, so that cost–push inflation comes down; and, bolster the animal spirits in the minds of producers and consumers through economic reforms which have remained on the backburner for quite some time. We have referred to these reforms separately in each of the previous chapters. Specifically, these involve:

1. Building up a consensus in Parliament and allowing multi-brand FDI in the retail sector. This would eliminate the cascading profit margins of the numerous middlemen in the supply chain. The elimination of middlemen—coupled with healthy competition between a few foreign retailers and well-established domestic chains—would keep the

price rise in check. This would also help send a signal to the private sector that economic reforms are on track.

2. Introducing a single GST at the earliest, so that the cascading effect (tax-on-tax, see Chapter 2) of the multiplicity of taxes and the attendant delays in the supply chain can be avoided, exerting a dampening effect on the price rise. The speedy implementation of GST would also send a positive signal to industry that the government meant business.

3. Expediting the disinvestment of public sector undertakings— an economic reform agenda that has long remained on the backburner. This will not only promote operational efficiency, but give a one-time boost to lower budget deficits at least for a few years.

4. Fast-track handling of the series of corruption and scam cases which will give a positive signal to industry that all businesses are treated fairly. This will go a long way towards reviving the animal spirits which seem to have dimmed somewhat at this time.

5. Publishing unemployment rates at regular intervals. Bringing out such statistics on a monthly or even quarterly basis is important as it helps various stakeholders to assess the economic situation frequently and to calibrate their policy initiatives.

6. Allowing private competition against monopolistic APMC wholesale markets dealing in agricultural produce. The competition would lower trader margins and keep price rise in check.

7. RBI engages in selective credit control, by making banks charge higher interest rates on working capital loans for private food warehouses, particularly when food price inflation raises its head again, and thereby discouraging the hoarding of food supplies.

8. Improving the output delivery of MGNREGS so that quality construction of bunds, roads, and wells would increase not only employment but agricultural productivity as well.

9. Infusing new technology into agriculture in the form of GM (genetically modified) foods; building up the agricultural infrastructure; lowering customs duties. Among others, these are the few steps required to meet the future demand, for population growth has outstripped growth in food grain production by an average of 0.2 percent per year for the past two decades.

## REFERENCES:

Basu, K., (2011), 'Capital is Going Abroad to Escape Bureaucracy', an interview with Dr Kaushik Basu in *India Today*, November 21

Government of India, (2011), 'Press Note: Key Indicators of Employment and Unemployment in India, 2009–10,' NSSO (National Sample Survey Office), Ministry of Statistics and Programme Implementation

———, (2010), 'Report on Employment and Unemployment Survey, 2009–10,' Ministry of Labour and Employment, Chandigarh, October 2010

Gupta, S., (2011), 'National Interest: That Sinking Feeling', in The

*Indian Express*, December 10, http://www.indianexpress.com/news/national-interest-that-sinking-feeling/886142/, accessed on 24-12-2011

Keynes, J., (1936), 'The General Theory of Employment, Interest and Money'. Reprint of the first edition, 1976, London: The Macmillan Press

Reserve Bank of India (RBI), (2011), 'RBI Annual Report 2010–11', http://www.rbi.org.in/scripts/Annual ReportPublications.aspx, accessed on 28-12-2011

United States Department of Labor, (2011), 'How the Government Measures Unemployment', Bureau of Labor Statistics, United States Department of Labour (USDL), http://www.bls.gov/cps/cps_htgm.htm, accessed on 23-12-2011

# READY RECKONER

**Animal Spirits:** Spontaneous optimism and urge to action among businesses, which is conditioned by the socio-economic and political environment. The term was used by John Maynard Keynes, the father of modern macroeconomics in his 1936 treatise, *The General Theory of Employment, Interest and Money.*

**Booms and Bust:** A term used to describe business cycles. See Business Cycle.

**Business Cycle:** A phenomenon in a free market economy where periods of high growth in GDP and employment are followed by a low or negative growth in GDP and employment.

**Cyclical Unemployment:** Unemployment associated with the business cycle or the boom and bust in the economy.

**Depression:** A severe form of recession. For example, GDP, employment, and prices fell by about 25 percent in the US during the period 1929 to 1933. This was referred to as the Great Depression.

**Fiscal Policy:** The policy adopted by the government of a country to alter its spending or taxes to bring changes to GDP, employment and inflation in the economy.

**Frictional Unemployment:** Unemployment that occurs when people happen to be between jobs or have just graduated from school.

**Involuntary Unemployment:** An activity status where individuals actively seek jobs at given wage rates but do not find one.

**Labour Force:** Those who are employed and involuntarily unemployed.

**Monetary Policy:** The policy adopted by the central bank of a country to change money supply to bring changes to GDP, employment and inflation in the economy.

**Natural Unemployment:** Unemployment that consists of the frictional and the structural types.

**Overheating of economy:** A phenomenon where business and consumer optimism lead to a higher demand for goods and services, resulting in a higher GDP growth rate, but, in which, the factors of production are overworked and this leads to inflation.

**Recession:** An economic phenomenon where GDP falls for at least two consecutive quarters. Quite often, a sharp fall in the GDP growth rate also gets described as recession.

**Stagflation:** An economic phenomenon characterized by high inflation and high unemployment.

**Structural Unemployment:** Unemployment caused by structural changes among various sub-sectors of the economy, leading to a mismatch between the vacancies and the skills in the labour force, until workers can be retrained or relocated.

**Unemployment Rate:** The percentage of labour force that is involuntarily unemployed.

**Voluntary Unemployment:** An activity status where individuals choose not to seek employment at the given wage rates.

# CHAPTER 7

# UNAIMED OPULENCE

*'Unaimed opulence, in general, is a roundabout, undependable, and wasteful way of improving the living standards of the poor.'*

—JEAN DRÈZE AND AMARTYA SEN

## INDIA, THE HUNKY-DORY STORY

India's story spanning a few millennia has been quite agreeable. The long road leading right up to this century has been paved with many successes and breakthroughs. After all, this is the country which gave the zero and the decimal system to the world. Many East Asian countries have shown an exemplary economic growth in the twentieth century. And, for centuries, these very countries have all been inspired by India with its philosophical heritage steeped in Buddhism and Hinduism. It is also this country, whose non-violent struggle for Independence has been emulated by several Asian and African countries. Today, India is the largest functioning democracy in the world. She is one of the very few countries to have developed a home-grown technology for atomic energy and weapons, and belongs to an exclusive and select group of countries that have initiated their own space exploration programmes.

According to the retrospective documentation by Angus Maddison, India's economy was the largest in the world between 1 CE and 1000 CE. However, history too, seems to go through business cycles—thereafter, India remained dormant, although restless, for almost a millennium. In fact, enmeshed in Nehruvian socialism—and the consequent tight controls on the private sector, imports and exports—the first three decades of India's Independence saw a sluggish growth in GDP. An average growth rate barely reaching 3.5 percent per year during this period is slammed and christened as the Hindu rate of growth by a few economists. However, since 1992, India's GDP growth rate has been phenomenal, averaging about 7.3 percent per year. The fiscal years 2009–10 and 2010–11 experienced an average annual GDP growth rate of about 9 percent, one of the best in the contemporary world. States, like Gujarat, have progressed at an even more rapid pace during the past decade. Gujarat's state GDP and agriculture sector both grew at an average rate of nearly 11 percent. Today, in absolute terms, the GDP of Rs 79 trillion in the fiscal year 2010–11 makes India the ninth largest economy in the world. And, according to PricewaterhouseCoopers, India will be the third largest economy in the year 2050. Already, according to the March 2011 edition of *Forbes* magazine, while a total of fifty-seven billionaires hailed from India, two had made their way to the list of world's top ten billionaires.

India's socio-political and economic story, narrated above in absolute numbers and in terms of recent growth figures, makes for quite a rosy picture. However, this isn't exactly a description of the current welfare of the majority of Indians, nor a culmination of their aspirations. While the GDP growth may generate employment and prosperity in general, the real issue is whether or not the prosperity and the opulence are shared by all, and how it affects ordinary people's lives. The GDP growth is expected to percolate through the layers of society, creating opportunities and capabilities among the population. It is important that, with a healthy growth rate and a prospering economy, adequate expertise and training be provided to achieve sustainable growth. To give a simple example, if a person is unable to develop a skill, say, cycling or swimming, then a bicycle or a swimming pool will be of little use to him/her. The development of profitable capabilities depends upon environmental conversion factors. The question is, can a high GDP growth provide these conversion factors?

## INDIA, THE CONTRARY STORY
### Anecdotal Experiences

Your housemaid generally comes on duty at the prescribed time. However, this may have more to do with her instinct or gut feeling than the ability to tell the time! Maybe, sometimes, you wish you could leave a written message for her to come at some other time if there is a change in your plans. The shortcoming in the execution of daily chores arises because the maid cannot read. Maybe, you are under tension when the driver of a hired car is supposed to pick you up at the airport. The name-placards which may, for example, read Ms Patil or Ms Patel, or Mr Nayyar or Mr Nair, are perhaps only images for the illiterate driver. You only hope that the driver has picked up the correct name-placard from among several pick-ups that he has been assigned to for the day. Even the standardized goods such as electrical fixtures and plastic gadgets suffer in quality since the unskilled labour force in India fails to stick to product specifications due to the lack of basic education.

Cleanliness in public places is maintained in the Western world more out of an observance of the social norms and the efficient waste management that have evolved within its society than out of a fear of draconian laws that are present in some totalitarian regimes. India—which seems to have neither—needs to have civic education, not meaningless learning by rote, imparted in primary and secondary schools. Children who learn to respect the environment and eschew littering will grow up to be responsible adults. Such basic education still eludes a significant proportion of children in India. Apart from sporadic wins in cricket and individual sports like chess and billiards, we sadly lag behind when it comes to competing in many international sports, including soccer, athletics, and swimming. And, for this, fingers are often pointed at poor standards of health, lack of stamina, food, and training.

Half-starving beggars knocking on your car window at a busy traffic light and malnourished children attempting to sell balloons to your kids sitting in the rear, are striking examples of people who lack basic health amenities and education. They are denied the opportunity to develop capabilities which would help them get work and obtain the ordinary necessities of life, and they are denied the right to live with dignity. These are extreme examples, but there are many in the continuum between the poorest of the poor and the not-so-destitute who may not be able to develop capabilities despite high growth rates in GDP. A congenial environment for development may be lacking, and GDP, as the sole measure of human well-being will not suffice to bring benefits to a large section of society. As Jean Drèze and Amartya Sen opined, unaimed opulence may be the result of such growth. Growth-mediated welfare may not trickle down—it might only make the rich richer and the poor, poorer.

## Quantitative Measures of the Contrary Story

While anecdotal experiences may provide a dramatic account of unaimed opulence, more serious observations can be drawn from quantitative data by comparing India with other countries on parameters other than GDP and its growth rate. While India may be ranked ninth in terms of the absolute level of GDP, this ranking becomes meaningless when we consider the per capita measure of GDP. In Table 7.1, we

### Table 7.1: Per Capita Gross National Income 2009 (US$)

| Norway | UK | Japan | S. Korea | S. Africa | China | India | Nepal |
|--------|-----|-------|----------|-----------|-------|-------|-------|
| 86,440 | 41,520 | 37,870 | 19,830 | 5,770 | 3,700 | 1,180 | 440 |

Source: *World Development Indicators* 2010

report the per capita Gross National Income (PC–GNI) of a few countries for illustrative purposes.[1] For 2009, Norway registered the highest per capita income of $86,440 and India, a paltry amount of $1180, only faring better than her neighbouring countries, such as, Nepal. China and South Korea were more or less in the same league as India at the time of India's Independence. However, in the last sixty years, China and, even more so, South Korea have leapfrogged in terms of PC–GNI in comparison to India.

PC–GNIs are expressed in terms of a single currency—the US dollar—for a meaningful comparison of incomes across countries. For example, in 2008–09, if India's PC–GNI were Rs 56,640 and the official exchange rate between the US dollar and the Indian rupee was $1 = Rs 48, then, in terms of the US dollars, India's PC–GNI would turn out to be $1180. With this calculation, the assumption is that one would have to spend $1 in the US to buy whatever goods and services Rs 48 would buy in India. However, the dollar–rupee exchange rate does not reflect the true purchasing power of the two

[1] GNI is a close cousin of GDP. It is arrived at by subtracting the net taxes paid (tax minus subsidy) and adding the net factor incomes of Indian citizens from abroad to GDP at market prices. Thus, GNI represents the income accruing to Indian citizens valued at factor cost.

currencies. This is because the exchange rate is determined only on the basis of the demand and supply of the two currencies that are required for import and export and for financial transactions. Moreover, besides these requirements, there are millions of other goods and services that are traded within each country but not between the two countries. Hence, the dollar–rupee exchange rate may not represent the true value of the purchasing power of the currencies within their respective domestic markets.

Therefore, the World Bank looks at what is called purchasing power parity (PPP) incomes. It determines the PPP every five years by obtaining and coordinating data regarding the prices of a basket of more than 1000 commodities from all countries through its International Comparison Programme (ICP), and identifying the PPP exchange rate of each country in relation to the US dollar. This exchange rate is used to calculate PC–GNI valued at the PPP exchange rate. Essentially, through the PPP exchange rate, ICP answers the question—how much local currency would be required for buying a given basket that may cost $1 in the US? For example, the official exchange rate between the Indian and the US currency may be $1 = Rs 48; but, based on PPP, it may turn out that only Rs 16 is needed to buy a basket of goods that can be bought for $1 in the US. Therefore, India's national income may turn out to be three times bigger than the one based on the official exchange rate. Table 7.2 presents the PC–GNI based on PPP for various countries for illustrative purpose.

### Table 7.2: PPP Per Capita Gross National Income 2009 (PPP in US$)

| Norway | UK | Japan | S. Korea | S. Africa | China | India | Nepal |
|--------|--------|--------|----------|-----------|-------|-------|-------|
| 56,050 | 37,360 | 33,280 | 27,310 | 10,060 | 6,700 | 3,260 | 1,100 |

Source: *World Development Indicators* 2010

From Table 7.2, we see that, with the PPP exchange rate, India's per capita income has jumped up to 3,260 PPP dollars while that of Norway has come down to 56,050. Indians may feel relieved that the real gap between the rich and the poor has narrowed after using the PPP exchange rate. Nevertheless, the fact remains that India is one of the poorest countries in the world in terms of the availability of goods and services per person. As for those who, during coffee-table conversations, are quick to blame India's bursting population as the reason for low incomes, there is a catch. When one talks of the burden of a large population, it is necessary to look at the density of the population, that is, the number of people per square kilometre area. Table 7.3 should open some eyes in this context. Although the density of India's population is high, it is still lower than that of South Korea, and yet, South Korea's per capita PPP income is almost nine times that of India. The population density of Japan is comparable to that of India, yet Japan's per capita PPP income is almost eleven times higher than that of India. Therefore, population by itself need not be a source of deprivation in India. As a nation, India has not fully exploited her potential in terms of generating a higher standard of living for an average Indian

### Table 7.3: Population Density (Persons per sq. km.)

| S. Korea | India | Japan | UK | Nepal | China | S. Africa | Norway |
|----------|-------|-------|-----|-------|-------|-----------|--------|
| 502 | 383 | 350 | 252 | 201 | 142 | 40 | 16 |

Source: *World Development Indicators* 2010

in terms of the volume, value, variety, and quality of goods and services.

Highly educated Indians—from the civil services, scientific establishments, IITs, IIMs, famous law schools, medical schools, leading universities and colleges of arts and humanities, and industry—probably believe, and rightly so, that they are in many ways more qualified than citizens of many other countries. But, unfortunately, this reality and perception of highly educated Indians is limited to a small minority of Indians who have access to education. If they were to look at the adult literacy rates among the East Asian countries which have had phenomenal and sustained high GDP growth rates for decades, and compare them to India, they would be shocked. World Bank figures for adult literacy rates, that is, the percentage of people aged fifteen and above who can, with understanding, read and write a short, simple statement about their everyday life, are as follows for a few countries.

### Table 7.4: Adult Literacy Rate (%)

| South Korea | | China | | Thailand | | India | |
|------|------|------|------|------|------|------|------|
| 1980 | 2008 | 1980 | 2008 | 1980 | 2008 | 1980 | 2008 |
| 93 | 98.3 | 69 | 94 | 68 | 94 | 36 | 63 |

Source: *World Development Indicators* 2010

South Korea had already begun its rapid economic growth prior to 1980 and, as depicted in Table 7.4, had almost universalized basic education by 1980 itself. Similarly, while China and Thailand were busy in their rapid economic growth starting 1980, it was accompanied by fruitful efforts to universalize basic education. In contrast, as recently as 2008, India's adult literacy rate was merely 63 percent, even lower than the low literacy rates in China and Thailand in 1980! This is evidence enough that we are far behind in terms of providing basic education to the people. The most recent population census data indicates that the literacy rate in India stands at 74 percent in 2011. This means that more than one in four still cannot read or write. Therefore, high GDP growth by itself is not sufficient to create opportunities for our citizens. Without universalization of basic education, it is difficult to develop the capabilities needed to be gainfully employed and to make a positive contribution to one's own, or the nation's, welfare. The apathy towards providing basic education and the inequality in its allocation are also perhaps making the population impatient—impatient to break the barriers and go further in the educational and professional fields. It should not come as a surprise, then, if there are ever-increasing demands from the disadvantaged communities for more reservation in educational institutions and employment.

Education aside, how well do we fare in the matter of health? One catch-all indicator that reflects the physical health of a society is the average life expectancy at birth. Table 7.5

gives the life expectancy at birth for a few countries for the year 2008. With a life expectancy of 80 years, South Korea is already in step with the developed world, and China is not far behind. India's life expectancy of 63.5 years is higher than that of Ethiopia, the famine-stricken and war-torn African nation. However, it is lower than that of its next-door neighbour, Nepal. Indeed, if we were to consider a few other health parameters, things do not look much brighter. For example, the latest census shows that, on an average, there are only 940 females per 1000 males nationwide. This number is as low as 901 in Madhya Pradesh, and 856 in places like Hardoi in Uttar Pradesh. Further, the Task Force Report on Micronutrients, by the Government of India, reported in 1996 that 69 percent of adolescent girls suffer from anaemia due to deficiency of iron and folic acid. While the above statistics are indicative of the gender bias in particular, they are also a reflection of poor education, a conservative attitude, and the low standard of health of Indians in general. Low female-to-male ratios and micronutrient deficiencies in girls show not only a preference for the male child, but also an alarming neglect of women's health. Importantly, enfeebled women give birth to weak children—boys and girls. It is also due to this reason that 67.5 percent of children below the age of five suffer from anaemia and iron deficiency. Such low levels of health standards contribute to malnourishment, ill health and morbidity in a significant proportion of the Indian population. And, ultimately, this affects the physical strength, stamina, work capabilities, and performance of the labour force.

**Table 7.5: Average Life Expectancy at Birth (Year 2008)**

| Japan | Norway | UK | S. Korea | China | Nepal | India | Ethiopia |
|-------|--------|------|----------|-------|-------|-------|----------|
| 82.5  | 80.5   | 80   | 80       | 73    | 66.5  | 63.5  | 54       |

Source: *World Development Indicators* 2010

Early implementation of land reforms is another factor that has contributed to the successful economic growth of some countries, such as, South Korea and China. The farming community has been able to improve its lot, for the land reforms prevented an excessive burden on employment in industry and gave incentive to small farmers to produce more. For example, in South Korea, land reforms started as early as 1945, when large lands held by the Japanese and the big Korean landlords were redistributed to peasants. In China, under the leadership of Mao Zedong, the Communist Party of China began a campaign in the late 1950s to transform China into a modern state through agrarian reforms and industrialization. Through this campaign—popularly known as the Great Leap Forward—all agricultural lands were collectivized by the government. However, the government soon realized that there was no individual incentive for farmers to produce more since all the surplus from farms went to the government. Therefore, in the 1970s, the government decided to give land-use rights to farmers whereby they could decide how much and what to produce on the farms. Farmers were required to produce a given minimum quota for the government, and they could sell out-of-quota produce in private markets and make a good income out of it. This system was successful in increasing the farm output and the farmers' income, and is known as the Household Responsibility System.

At the time of Independence in 1947, India inherited the system of land tenure and ownership developed during the colonial period. To ensure control over agriculture and tax revenues, the British had created a class of *zamindar*s and middlemen who had acquired ownership rights to huge tracts of lands, and who were responsible for collecting land revenue from farmer tenants and landless farmers. Vast tracts in the possession of zamindars and middlemen remained uncultivated. Moreover, there was also no incentive for the landless and the tenant farmers to make investments in farm improvement. Since they did not own the lands and they could get evicted at any time by the zamindars, they did not attempt constructing wells, bunds, and introducing new methods of cultivation. This had obstructed growth in agricultural production and in sufficient income generation for the landless and the tenant farmers.

To correct this situation, the government initiated land reform policies immediately after gaining Independence. The Land Reforms Act of India, 1955, and the subsequent Land Ceiling Acts passed in all the states aimed at eliminating the zamindari system; preventing the arbitrary eviction of tenants; putting a ceiling on the amount of land a household could own; and redistributing the surplus land to the landless. The zamindari system was abolished through these acts. Various states limited the landholding to between four and twenty-four hectares per household—depending upon whether or not the land was self-cultivated, irrigated, and could take one or two crops. The land in excess of these limits was to be taken possession of and redistributed by the government to the landless. However, the actual implementation of the policy was quite lacklustre. The late Vinoba Bhave, a devout Gandhian, began his Bhoodan (land donation) movement by criss-crossing the hinterlands of India, appealing to the conscience of the landed community to donate land voluntarily. However this, too, met with very little success. What was donated was mostly barren tracks of land. Perhaps this limited success of the land reforms policy has prevented small farmers and agricultural labourers from having sufficient incentives to produce more, and has led them to throng to the cities for work.

An important exception to the dismal human development indicators presented above is the success story of the state of Kerala. Its land reforms, introduced by the democratically elected communist government in 1957, were followed equally keenly by its successive state governments. Perhaps it is for this reason that the data from the NSSO 59th Round for 2003 shows that while the percentage of landless rural households was barely 4.7 in Kerala it was as high as 17.7 in Maharashtra. The initiatives undertaken by the state on health and education, too, were impressive. Earlier, we have presented India's average adult literacy rate and life expectancy at birth for the year 2008; the corresponding figures for Kerala were 98 percent and 74 years, respectively!

These figures are comparable to those of developed countries and East Asian countries. In fact, land reforms were also successful in West Bengal after 1977, the year when the communist government came into power. By the early 1980s, the Government of West Bengal ensured the security of the sharecroppers' tenancy rights. These two examples suggest that, if the other state governments had been similarly sincere, land reforms could have been a success in those states as well. However, unfortunately, both the states have had market-unfriendly governments for quite some time now and, hence, they have apparently failed to achieve GDP-growth-mediated economic progress.

The state of Gujarat has demonstrated a high GDP-growth-mediated development during the last decade. Perhaps, a proactive focus on infrastructure, irrigation, spread of power grid, and good governance has paid dividends there. A state like Kerala—which has already achieved high levels in many of the human development indicators—may want to focus on this type of development to enhance further the employment opportunities in the state. On the other hand, while most of the other states continue their GDP-growth-mediated development, the national averages on human development indicators reported above tell a contradictory story—they are very poor. To emphasize the point further, let us consider the infant mortality rate (IMR) provided in Table 7.6. IMR is defined as the number of infant (one year of age or younger) deaths per 1000 live births. Gujarat, a high-GDP-growth state, had a high IMR of 50 in the year 2008. Madhya Pradesh

### Table 7.6: Infant Mortality Rate (2008)

| Madhya Pradesh | Gujarat | China | Sri Lanka | Kerala | UK | Japan |
|---|---|---|---|---|---|---|
| 70 | 50 | 18 | 13 | 12 | 5 | 3 |

Source: *World Development Indicators* 2010; *Economic Survey* 2011

performed much worse with an IMR of 70 for the same year. The corresponding numbers for China, Sri Lanka, the Indian state of Kerala, UK, and Japan were, 18, 13, 12, 5, and 3, respectively. Clearly, unless improvements in human development indicators with government support are achieved, a simple GDP growth may result in unaimed opulence.

## SUPPORT-LED DEVELOPMENT

Improvement in the welfare and the development of a society occur due to two factors. One is the invisible hand of the market. The market-driven growth in GDP is expected to percolate through various sections of society. However, as discussed in Chapter 1, market failures do occur. In brief, when social benefits exceed private benefits—in that there are positive externalities—the market may under-provide certain services. For example, the benefit accruing to society by providing basic education to a girl child far outweighs the private benefit perceived by the girl or her family. Similarly, the societal benefits of offering vaccination and primary health care to an individual are far greater than the benefit accruing to the individual recipient. That is so because such services bring improvement in human capital, prevent communicable diseases, and improve labour force productivity. The private sector may not be in a position to offer such services to all and that, too, at affordable prices, unless their costs are subsidized or the government itself offers these services. Therefore, the improvement and the development of welfare depend upon government support. In fact, improvement in human development indicators through government support becomes a necessary condition for a universal reach of GDP-growth-mediated development.

The statistics provided in the previous section on human development indicators show that a high and fast GDP growth rate may be one of the methods for improving the welfare of society, but that, by itself, may not suffice. Indian experience shows that, irrespective of which political party is running the country, one tends to view with suspicion the various developmental schemes of the government. While there may be issues related to the implementation of the welfare schemes, the above discussion brings out the seriousness of the situation, and the urgency to implement them. In fact, society may want to capitalize on the growing strength of the Indian economy to engage in a support-led developmental strategy. We summarize below a few of the initiatives that have been undertaken by the Central government in conjunction with the state governments.

## Government Support to Education and Health

Even six decades after India achieved Independence, the universalization of primary and secondary education remains only a dream. Children are deprived of the basic education which should be imparted to them as their birthright. The Indian government has recognized and enforced this right by providing free education for all children between the ages of six to fourteen as a Fundamental Right. The Right to Education (RTE) Act has come into force from April 1, 2010. With this Act, imparting basic education to children has become a duty and responsibility of the state. To further this objective, the government is adopting various schemes to promote basic education. For example, schemes, such as the Sarva Shiksha Abhiyan (SSA) and the Kasturba Gandhi Balika Vidyalaya, have been introduced in a concerted drive for the benefit of disadvantaged communities and children. The aim is to provide new schools, buildings, books, and trained teachers at the primary and secondary education levels. The Central government had allocated a total of Rs 1500 crores for SSA for the fiscal year 2010–11.

Another novel initiative that has been going on for a few decades but was strengthened recently is the National Programme of Nutrition Support to Primary Education (NP-NSPE), popularly known as the Midday Meal Scheme. The government offers this programme, whereby children in class I–VIII in state-aided schools are provided with cooked meals in school at lunch time—as an incentive to disadvantaged children to come to school. This also gives them the dual advantage of learning and having nutritious food that contains essential micronutrients, such as, iron, folic acid and vitamin A. In effect, the scheme is expected to have a four-

## Oliverian Twist to Midday Meal Scheme

In pre-British India, *annachhatras* (charity dining halls) were patronized by royalty and the rich to feed the needy. In England, the passing of the Poor Law Amendment Act of 1834 emphasized the importance of 'workhouses' as a means of giving food relief to the poor. The philosophical basis for the act was guided by the utilitarian ideas of Jeremy Bentham (1748–1832), known for his axiom, 'it is the greatest happiness of the greatest number that is the measure of right and wrong.' However, the actual problems encountered in the running of the workhouses are movingly narrated by Charles Dickens in his novel, *Oliver Twist*. Nine-year-old Oliver, like the other residents, was entitled to 'three meals of thin gruel a day, with an onion twice a week, and half a roll on Sundays'. Not getting their due share, the starving children held a council and it fell upon Oliver to famously ask, 'Please, sir, I want some more.' The above accounts show that historically, society had recognized hunger and basic health as a market failure, and tried to make provision for such public good either through private charity or public policy.

A similar public policy initiative was lifted up a couple of notches in India by linking it to primary education when the-then Madras Corporation developed a school lunch programme in 1925, the first ever to do so. In the post-Independence era, the state of Gujarat started a school lunch programme in 1984. However, it was only in 1995 that the NP–NSPE was launched at the national level. Popularly known as the Midday Meal Scheme, the objective of this programme was to give a boost to the universalization of primary education and to impact the nutritional intake of students in primary classes. As per the latest norms of the programme, government-aided schools are mandated to provide cooked meals on at least 200 days with adequate provision of micronutrients, such as, iron, folic acid and vitamin A. For upper primary students, each meal must provide a minimum content of 700 calories and 20 grams of protein.

A study conducted to find out the nutritional quality of the cooked meal suggests that the protein and other micronutrient contents of the meal in the tested samples were very low. Perhaps this was related to the rations supplied from the old stocks coming from the Food Corporation of India (FCI) and perhaps also to the non-standardized, watered-down preparations that may not contain as much nutrition as expected and desired. A planning commission report on the evaluation of the Midday Meal Scheme also points out to the possibilities of adulteration and pilferage of supplies. The government has to pay attention to these lacunae by ensuring provision of quality foodgrains and standardized recipes. If a modern-day Oliver could measure the nutrition content in the cooked meals, he would perhaps ask for a more nutritious meal. In fact, the delivery of meals and nutrition can be improved if packaged foods, such as, *chikki* and *sukhdi* and an occasional nutrition bar, are supplied a few times a week to complement the cooked meal. As part of corporate social responsibility, help from the food industry by way of supplying the same can also be sought.

fold benefit for poor children—food, nutrition, education, and shelter for the brief period that they spend in the school premises. The Central government had allocated Rs 9,440 crores for this scheme for the fiscal year 2010–11.

In the year 2005, the Government of India also initiated the National Rural Health Mission (NRHM) to provide accessible and affordable healthcare services to rural areas. In addition, state governments, too, have initiated their own health schemes. For example, in September 2006, the Gujarat government introduced the Chiranjeevi Scheme for below-the-poverty-line (BPL) families and tribal communities in all districts. Through this service, the state government offers child-birth support and pre- and post-natal health services to disadvantaged households. It is heartening to know that, in the year 2009, Gujarat's Chiranjeevi Scheme was awarded the Asian Innovations Award by the *Wall Street Journal*, and also the Prime Minister's Award. It may not come as a surprise that the latest Sample Registration Survey Report by the Registrar General of India shows that in just two years the IMR for Gujarat has come down from 50 in 2008 to 44 in 2010. Of course, Gujarat still has a long way to go, for the IMR figures for Tamil Nadu, Maharashtra, and Delhi were 24, 28 and 30 respectively for the year 2010.

## Employment Guarantee

While one of the main aims of fiscal policy is to reduce the high unemployment rate, the policy is, essentially, a short-term measure for tackling the boom-and-bust phenomenon.

However, governments may go beyond providing these short-term cushions to reduce unemployment. To bring certain sections of society out of the chronic cycle of low incomes, poor education, low health status, and low employability, governments may provide jobs to rural folks to promote inclusive growth. EGS, the very first such successful scheme was implemented in Maharashtra in the 1970s. On the same lines, the Government of India initiated the MGNREGS, which is, today, its flagship programme aiming at inclusive growth. The MGNREGS Act, which has been notified throughout the country since April 1, 2008, aims at providing livelihood security in rural areas by ensuring at least 100 days of work in one year to every household whose adult members volunteer to do unskilled manual work. For the fiscal year 2010–11, the Central government had allocated Rs 40,000 crore for this programme. The efficacy of this programme will depend, however, not just on full and proper disbursement of these funds, but also on the development of quality, permanent asset creation; build-up of infrastructure through rural works; and providing employment during the non-sowing and non-harvesting seasons.

## Land Reforms

As mentioned earlier, land reforms have not been a success in India except in a few states. As per the NSSO 59th Round in the year 2003, about 80 percent of rural households (all marginal farmers) accounted for only 23 percent of the land ownership. On the other hand, 4 percent of medium and large farmer households with 4 hectares or more of land each, owned about 35 percent of the landholdings. From the previous reforms, about two million acres of land in various states already exists as land declared 'surplus', but has not yet been distributed due to court litigations. Thus, there is some potential for enforcing land ceiling acts. Moreover, many states have banned the leasing of agricultural land, and whatever leasing exists is on an informal basis. As a result, small farmers do not have any incentive to cultivate unused lands. Allowing the leasing of agricultural land may improve the rural folks' source of income. If one is to go by recent media reports, the central minister for rural development is keen to reduce the landholdings of absentee landlords to half the existing norms. However, having said this, further land reforms seem a difficult and distant possibility due to the political infeasibility and the growing realization that even if lands were redistributed now, the ever-increasing population would reduce the average per capita landholding.

## SEIZE THE OPPORTUNITY

After attaining Independence in 1947, Indian leaders were once again able to reaffirm their pride in the country's ancient civilization and design a newly found socialistic pattern of society for a glorious future. However, the socio-economic performance of the first four decades seemed disheartening. Of course, while one could showcase quite a few landmark events as proofs of achievements, the economic growth—particularly the growth rate of GDP—had turned out to be extremely modest. On the other hand, many East Asian economies zoomed past India with astonishing rates of GDP growth. While we have been considering South Korea as a yardstick in this chapter—it has almost turned into a developed nation— the stories of Taiwan, Hong Kong, Thailand, Indonesia, and Malaysia are similar, though in varying degrees. In fact, from the 1980s onwards, China began to bloom in full glory. And, from the point of view of civilization, these were the very countries which had received inspiration from Indian philosophical thought centuries ago.

As brought out in the previous sections, the necessary conditions for growth-mediated development, that is, high levels of human development indicators, in most of these countries, were achieved prior to their economic liberalization. These necessary conditions include, mainly, the universalization of basic education, a betterment of physical health through primary health care, and land reforms. One could have discounted the failure to achieve high growth rates in India if only she had been busy universalizing basic education, health care, and equitable land distribution. After all, communist Cuba did just that. But, despite the socialistic pattern of society that was aimed at, India failed in this task as well. It is only in the last two decades, starting with 1991, that we have shown a substantive economic resilience in terms of GDP growth rates. However, a high GDP and its growth cannot be an end in itself. It is only a means to achieve higher welfare for the common man.

If high growth could trickle down, this would be welcome. However, we must remember that, unlike East Asian economies, we have not put the necessary conditions in place. Hence, government-support-mediated improvement in human development indicators is critical. Now, with high GDP growth rates, we at least have the luxury to plan and spend money for support-mediated development. Therefore, the success of various programmes, including—but not limited to—the Midday Meal Scheme, SSA, the NRHM, and projects such as Chiranjeevi of the Gujarat state, is extremely critical. Attaining the universalization of necessary conditions, such as, health and education, will give opportunities to people to do things that they want to do and do them right and, in the process, raise their standard of living. India must avoid a singular focus on GDP growth as also the profligate management of government programmes. It must seize the opportunity and avoid unaimed opulence.

## REFERENCES:

Deodhar, S., Mahandiratta, S., Ramani, K., Mavalankar, D., Ghosh, S. and Braganza, V., (2011), 'An Oliverian Twist to Evaluation of Midday Meal Scheme', project paper of the Centre for Management of Health Services, Indian Institute of Management, Ahmedabad

Drèze, J. and Sen, A., (1989), *Hunger and Public Action*, Oxford: Clarendon Press

Maddison, A., (2007), *Contours of the World Economy, 1–2030 AD: Essays in Macro-Economic History,* New York: Oxford University Press

Government of India, (2011), '*Economic Survey*, 2010–11', Ministry of Finance, Government of India (GOI), February, New Delhi: Oxford University Press

Haque, T., (2011), 'Improving the Rural Poors' Access to Land in India', document prepared by the Council for Social Development, for the Governance Knowledge Centre (GKC), http://indiagovernance. gov.in/docsearch.php?search=haque&x=0&y=0 accessed on January 12, 2012

Hawksworth, J. and Tiwari, A., (2011), *The World in 2050*, PwC economics practice, http://www.pwc.com/en_GX/gx/world-2050/ pdf/world-in-2050-jan-2011.pdf, PricewaterhouseCoopers

Robeyns, R., (2005), 'The Capabilities Approach: A Theoretical Survey.' *Journal of Human Development*, 6(1), pp. 93–114

Stanton, E., (2007), 'The Human Development Index: A History', Working Paper Series, No. 127, Political Economy Research Institute, Amherst: University of Massachusetts

# READY RECKONER

**Adult Literacy Rate:** The percentage of people aged fifteen and above who can, with understanding, read and write a short, simple statement about their everyday life.

**Infant Mortality Rate:** The number of infants dying before reaching one year of age, per 1000 live births in a given year.

**Life Expectancy at Birth:** The number of years that a newborn infant would live if the patterns of mortality prevailing at the time of its birth were to stay the same throughout its life.

**PPP Exchange Rate:** The exchange rate based on the purchasing power parity (PPP). It measures the amount of local currency required to purchase a certain basket of goods that $1 would purchase in the US.

# CHAPTER 8

# ECOLOGUE

*'I don't see novels ending with any real sense of closure.'*

—MICHAEL ONDAATJE

## THE ROOKIE'S GUIDE

Adi Shankaracharya, the eighth-century saint, poet, and philosopher, engaged himself in scholarly debates with monks from different parts of India. During one of his journeys in the north, he had a debate with Mandan Mishra, the renowned scholar. Bharati, wife of Mandan Mishra, and a scholar in her own right, was to act as referee and give the verdict on whose ideas and logic prevailed. According to the terms of the debate, the one who lost would become the other's disciple. As expected, Mandan Mishra was outsmarted by Adi Shankaracharya but the referee refused to give a verdict! Bharati challenged Adi Shankaracharya to a debate, arguing that, unlike him, Mandan Mishra was a *grihastha*, that is, a householder, and therefore, the debate could not be over until he had engaged her in a scholarly verbal duel. Adi Shankaracharya agreed but soon found that he was at a loss when it came to issues related to conjugal responsibilities and pleasures. He told Bharati that, being celibate as he was, he needed time to imbibe the experiences of a gruhastha. Bharati agreed to grant him a month's time. Adi Shankaracharya, through his yogic powers, entered the body of a king to experience the conjugal responsibilities and pleasures, returned to the debate and won.

You might wonder what this has to do with day to day economics. Well, we all specialize in our own various areas of interest and profession, and devote time to them. Whether as a dedicated school teacher, a software programmer, a manager in a steel company, a civil engineer in a construction company, or any other professional—one rarely gets time to focus on the nitty-gritty of day to day economics. Nonetheless, the fact of the matter is that one has to take many decisions taking into account the business environment in which one lives. Therefore, it makes sense to take a short and quick break to understand economics. And, like Adi Shankaracharya, one does not have much time on hand. Hopefully, this book will have served a purpose towards that end. Through it, we have attempted to give exposure to the institutions, phenomena, and principles that guide the working of the economic environment.

Of course, it is more likely than not, that the purists will assert that the description of the economic issues is neither complete nor very precise. But then, this is a 'rookie's guide' to the Indian economy. It has been fashioned to overcome the perceived inaccessibility of economics to consumers and businesses alike. Adi Shankaracharya did not have the luxury of experiencing the full life of a king, but he did gain sufficient knowledge to fight successfully the challenge posed by Bharati. Similarly, this rookie's guide does not have the luxury of presenting the full spectrum of the various nuances of economic thought, but, it does provide sufficient knowledge about day to day economics to help a non-expert understand. The path of the earth around the sun is not elliptical. However, the exposition of celestial phenomena, such as, the occurrence of seasons, the phases of the moon, and the eclipses, can be easily understood by assuming that it is elliptical. This book should be understood in that context.

## A QUICK ROUND-UP

We started this book by posing a myriad everyday economic questions. You now probably have more than a cursory inkling about the answers to those questions, for you have become familiar with quite a few important institutions and phenomena that affect our economic life. For example, you can now understand better the inflation rates quoted by the government and the media—whether it is a headline inflation quote or a CPI inflation quote. After a series of increases in the repo rate, if RBI reverses its policy by resorting to an expansionary monetary policy—also known as 'quantitative easing' or 'pumping liquidity'—you will infer that the inflationary pressure must have been reduced significantly.

And, therefore, you may expect interest rates to come down. Similarly, when global economies, including India's, pass through times of recession, such as the one that began in the year 2007, you can expect governments to reduce tax rates. The idea is that a reduction in tax rates would incentivize producers and consumers to generate more demand for goods and services, in turn improving the unemployment situation that is associated with recession.

On the other hand, governments cannot adopt expansionary polices in a profligate manner for that would lead to high fiscal deficits. Cumulative high fiscal deficits would lead to chronic internal and external debt, and difficulties in repayment could cause economic hardships as witnessed recently by some European countries, particularly Greece. We also know that high fiscal deficits crowd out private investments, and that wasteful public expenditure causes inflation. Therefore, it is very critical that budget allocations on MGNREGS, the Midday Meal Scheme, SSA, Chiranjeevi, and a host of other policies, be spent judiciously to ensure creation of permanent, quality rural assets, universalization of education, and improved health care. Other crucial subsidies on food, fuel, and fertilizers are difficult to eliminate in the short run, for they are politically sensitive. They can only be eased out in the long run. Since curbing expenditure on subsidies is a difficult task for the government, the deficit can also be kept in control by fiscal consolidation through revenue generation. Till as late as 1994, services were not taxed in India. Currently, the number of services included under indirect taxation is about 117 and this number is expected to grow. If the business services you offer have not yet been brought under the service tax regime, you may expect that, sooner or later, they will be. The introduction of GST is also expected to be implemented very soon. GST will avoid multiplicity of taxes and their cascading effects, making tax administration less cumbersome. This will promote business activities, tax compliance, and revenues collection.

Yet another feature that will help limit fiscal deficits and, more importantly, eliminate the excessive intrusion by the government into the marketplace, is the disinvestment of public sector enterprises. Circa 2000, the Indian government did privatize companies, such as, Modern Food Industries, Paradeep Phosphates, and Bharat Aluminium Company, but the process of disinvestment has slowed down considerably thereafter. Recall the discussion in Chapter 1, where we identified the cases in which the government should undertake an economic activity. They were the economic activities characterized by non-rivalry in consumption and excludability. Air India—which keeps accumulating losses amounting to thousands of crores of rupees—does not seem to fit into this characterization. In fact, Australia, Canada, and the UK have, in the past, privatized Australian Airlines, Air Canada, and British Airways, respectively. The Indian government may want to bring the privatization initiative to the fore once again.

In Chapter 4, we observed that on the international trade front, significant liberalization has occurred under the auspices of WTO. The current Doha Round of trade negotiations is yet to be concluded. The global recession is, perhaps, preventing countries from committing themselves to further liberalization. However, the trade liberalization process is sure to go only one way—the eventual lowering of customs duties, export and domestic subsidies, and the harmonization of intellectual property rights. In fact, many countries are now lowering trade barriers among themselves by forming free trade areas. Hopefully, these will eventually get extended to all member countries of WTO. Liberalization will not be restricted to trade alone. Allowing for a substantive share of foreign investments in multi-brand retail will help us develop a professionally managed supply chain, create competition among several foreign and domestic retail chains, and avoid the cascading effects of middlemen margins. This will result in consumers receiving quality products at competitive prices.

In the chapter dealing with the boom and the bust phenomena, we noted that providing a congenial environment for business and customers is important to help an economy avoid slipping into recession. Events, such as, the introduction and quick roll-back of policies on foreign investment in multi-brand retailing; a perceived delay in the introduction of the GST system; the sequential recurrences of corruption scams including, but not limited to, Adarsh Housing Society; CWG (Commonwealth Games); Spectrum 2G; and the resultant movement by Anna Hazare—all lead to the dimming of the proverbial animal spirits in the economy. Such pessimism in the market tends to reduce investments and hamper growth in the economy. Hopefully, these events will not be the order of the day; and proactive, transparent, credible, and stable policies will emerge, providing a congenial environment to businesses and customers alike.

Of course, it has been evident, during the last decade in general and the past few years in particular, that India's GDP growth rate has been quite phenomenal. In the midst of the current worldwide recession and the uncertain domestic environment, the slowdown of the Indian economy has been minimal. Now, the new floor for the-then pejorative 'Hindu rate of growth' has perhaps reached 7 percent. As discussed in the previous chapter, the challenge now is to avoid unaimed opulence. As months and years go by, many of us keep upgrading our cell phones, iPods, iPads, or move on to newer gadgets. Picture yourself at a busy intersection, awaiting the green signal, using these very gadgets. Someone may knock on your car window—a haggard child in worn-out clothes, or a poor pregnant woman, selling balloons or merely begging. At that time, instead of pretending they don't exist, we must ask ourselves a question—if land reforms were successful and universalization of health care and basic education were achieved, would this child or woman still be here at the crossroads? In fact, it is we who are at the crossroads—how soon can we universalize primary health care and how soon can we universalize basic education, so that a child or a woman like this would not have to knock on our car windows?

Michael Ondaatje, the Booker Prize-winning novelist, opined that he does not see novels ending with any real sense of closure. The same is true of this book. We have introduced ourselves to the workings of a few economic institutions and phenomena. I hope by now the curiosity and interest in the subject of economics—often wrongly dubbed as a dismal science—has been aroused. The intent of this book is not to bring a closure to the understanding of Indian economy and everyday economics, but to equip you to understand, reflect, and make informed decisions as and when you encounter new situations. You may specialize in your own field. You may be an artist, a homemaker, a programmer, an engineer, a student, or a zoologist, but you may not have time to be an economist. Like Adi Shankaracharya's quick attempt to understand the life of a householder, reading this book can be your quick attempt to get up close and personal with economics. Your journey as an everyday economist has just begun. Bon voyage!

As we part, if you want to get some self-accreditation, solve the following crossword puzzle.

## Crossword Puzzle

---

### ACROSS

5. This concept shows India's per capita income about 3 times larger than her per capita income measured in US dollars (3).

### DOWN

1. Other things remaining the same, this will get reduced as the government adopts fiscal consolidation (7).

| ACROSS | DOWN |
|---|---|
| 6. This man, known as the father of modern economics, wrote a treatise on the wealth of nations in 1776 (5). | 2. Opulence that is characterized by high economic growth but low human development indicators (7). |
| 7. A WTO principle of non-discrimination among trading nations which is often misunderstood due to its wording (3). | 3. Value of final goods and services produced in a given period within the territorial boundaries of a country (3). |
| 8. A negative impact of this leads to market failure, which the government tries to correct by levying green taxes on pollution and sin taxes on alcohol (11). | 4. RBI policy for controlling inflation or unemployment (8). |
| 11. Inflation in wholesale prices that ignores prices of fuel and food (4). | 6. A minimum percentage of net demand and time liabilities that banks are mandated by RBI to maintain in the form of government securities, gold, and cash on hand (3). |
| 12. A policy rate controlled by RBI to influence short-term liquidity and money supply (4). | 9. An economist and also a U-shaped curve that relates tax rates to tax revenue (6). |
| 14. This kind of equity is achieved when those who are equal are taxed equally (10). | 10. This is how inflation based on the wholesale price index is described (8). |
| 15. Unemployment in the economy that is associated with economic boom and bust (8). | 13. Expansionary policy followed by the government to cure unemployment (6). |

| ACROSS | DOWN |
|---|---|
| 18. No one offers this service in the private sector. Without exception, this is a classic case of pure public good (7). | 16. This is how an excludable and non-rival good is described (4). |
| 20. These duties are applied on imported goods (7). | 17. Index of 30 sensitive and actively traded shares on the Bombay Stock Exchange (6). |
| | 19. A minimum percentage of net demand and time liabilities that banks are mandated by RBI to maintain in the form of cash (3). |

# A NOTE ON THE AUTHOR

Satish Y. Deodhar teaches economics at the Indian Institute of Management, Ahmedabad (IIMA). After pursuing his bachelor's and master's degrees in economics at the Gokhale Institute of Politics and Economics, Pune, and at The Ohio State University (OSU), USA, he received his PhD in agricultural economics at OSU. A recipient of the Outstanding PhD Dissertation Award from the Food Distribution Research Society, USA, and of the Distinguished Young Professor Award for Excellence in Research from IIMA, he has worked on imperfectly competitive market structures, agricultural trade, World Trade Organization (WTO), and food quality issues. Professor Deodhar was selected as a Fellow of the Hewlett–IATRC Capacity Building Program in Agricultural Trade Policy during 2006–08. He has conducted consulting projects for Indian Bank; Ministry of Food Processing Industries, Government of India; and the Economic Research Service of the United States Department of Agriculture.

Several of his research studies have been conducted for the Ministry of Agriculture, Government of India. At IIMA, he has served as Warden, PGP Admissions Chairperson, and was the first Convener of the computerized Common Admission Test (CAT) of the Indian Institutes of Management. Currently, he chairs the PGPX programme.

# A NOTE ON IIMA BUSINESS BOOKS

The IIM Ahmedabad Business Books series brings key issues in management and business to a general audience. With a wealth of information and illustrations from contemporary Indian business, these non-academic and user-friendly books from the faculty of IIM Ahmedabad are essential corporate reading.

www.iimabooks.com

# OTHER BOOKS IN THIS SERIES

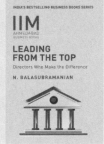